Listening and Responding

Managerial Communication Series

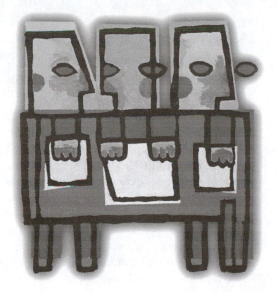

By **Sandra D. Collins**
University of Notre Dame

Series Editor: **James S. O'Rourke, IV**
University of Notre Dame

THOMSON

SOUTH-WESTERN

Australia · Brazil · Canada · Mexico · Singapore · Spain · United Kingdom · United States

THOMSON

SOUTH-WESTERN

Listening and Responding, Managerial Communication Series

James S. O'Rourke, IV, series editor; Sandra D. Collins, author

VP/Editorial Director:
Jack W. Calhoun

VP/Editor-in-Chief:
Dave Shaut

Sr. Publisher:
Melissa Acuna

Acquisitions Editor:
Neil Marquardt

Sr. Developmental Editor:
Taney Wilkins

Sr. Marketing Manager:
Larry Qualls

Production Editor:
Robert Dreas

Manager of Technology, Editorial:
Vicky True

Web Coordinator:
Scott Cook

Manufacturing Coordinator:
Diane Lohman

Production House:
Lachina Publishing Services

Printer:
Transcontinental
Louiseville, Quebec

Art Director:
Stacy Shirley

Cover and Internal Designer:
Robb and Associates

Cover Images:
© Artville/Richard Cook

Library of Congress Control Number:
2005928322

For more information about our
products, contact us at:
Thomson Learning
Academic Resource Center
1-800-423-0563

Thomson Higher Education
5191 Natorp Boulevard
Mason, OH 45040
USA

AUTHOR BIOGRAPHIES

Sandra Dean Collins currently teaches management communication for the Mendoza College of Business at the University of Notre Dame. Her courses include business writing, speaking, listening and responding, and managing differences. She has also taught statistics and research methods for the university. She conducts team training for the Mendoza College of Business and local organizations and consults with small and mid-size organizations on communication and team-related issues. Her background includes a Ph.D. in Social Psychology and experience in sales, purchasing, and banking.

James S. O'Rourke teaches management and corporate communication at the University of Notre Dame, where he is Founding Director of the Eugene D. Fanning Center for Business Communication and Concurrent Professor of Management. In a career spanning four decades, he has earned an international reputation in business and corporate communication. *Business Week* magazine has twice named him one of the "outstanding faculty" in Notre Dame's Mendoza College of business.

His publications include *Management Communication: A Case-Analysis Approach* from Prentice-Hall, now in second edition, and *Business Communication: A Framework for Success* from Thomson Learning. Professor O'Rourke is also senior editor of an eight-book series on Managerial Communication and is principal author or directing editor of more than 100 management and corporate communication case studies.

Professor O'Rourke is a graduate of Notre Dame with advanced degrees from Temple University, the University of New Mexico, and a Ph.D. in Communication from the S. I. Newhouse School of Syracuse University. He has held faculty appointments at the United States Air Force Academy, the Defense Information School, the United States Air War College, and the Communications Institute of Ireland. He was a Gannett Foundation Teaching Fellow at Indiana University in the 1980s, and a graduate student in language and history at Christ's College, Cambridge University in England during the 1970s.

Professor O'Rourke is a member and trustee of The Arthur W. Page Society, and a member of the Reputation Institute and the Management Communication Association. He is also a regular consultant to *Fortune 500* and mid-size businesses throughout North America.

TABLE OF CONTENTS

Managerial Communication Series

Editor: James S. O'Rourke, IV

*The **Managerial Communication Series** is a series of modules designed to teach students how to communicate and manage in today's competitive environment. Purchase only this module as a supplemental product for your Business Communication, Management, or other Business course, or purchase all eight modules, packaged together at a discounted price for full coverage of Managerial Communication.*

ISBN: **0-324-15254-X**

This text reviews the latest research on small group and team interaction, and offers practical advice on project management, intra-team conflict, and improving results. It contains group and team worksheets, progress reports, and sample reporting instruments, as well as classroom discussion questions and case studies.

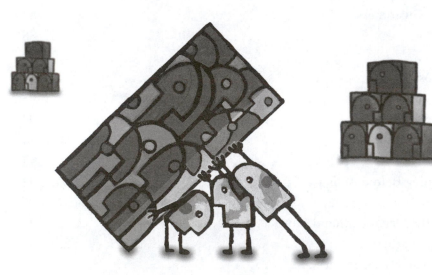

ISBN: **0-324-15257-4**

Learn what social scientists and business executives now know about conflict, personality style, organizational structure, and human interaction. Examine the most successful strategies for keeping your edge and keeping your friends. Practical forms, instruments, and applications are included.

*Contact your local Thomson Representative at 800-423-0563. Or visit the series Web site at **http://orourke.swlearning.com** for more product information and availability.*

e-Technology and the Fourth Economy
Carolyn A. Boulger

2 Managerial Communication Series | Editor: James S. O'Rourke, IV

ISBN: **0-324-15255-8**

This text offers a radical new view of technology's impact on what the author calls "The Fourth Economy," an economic model based entirely on minds in interaction. Technology's role in helping participants in the radically transformed landscape of the twenty-first century is not limited to the transmission and storage of text and data, but extends to the very ways in which people think about and create value.

Communication in a Virtual Organization
Sandra D. Collins

3 Managerial Communication Series | Editor: James S. O'Rourke, IV

ISBN: **0-324-15256-6**

This text explores the risks and opportunities open to those who work in new alliances, partnerships, and non-traditional business models. A look at both theory and practical application offers students and managers the chance to observe successful organizations in action. Foreword by Sixtus J. Oeschle of Shell Oil and Internet Pipeline.

Graphics and Visual Communication for Managers
Robert P. Sedlack, Jr.
Barbara L. Shwom
Karl P. Keller

4 Managerial Communication Series | Editor: James S. O'Rourke, IV

ISBN: **0-324-16178-6**

This text offers some practical and useful advice on how to work with graphics and visuals in reports, briefings, and proposals. It also offers direct instruction on how to integrate graphic aids into spoken presentations and public speeches. If you can't say it or write it clearly, you may be able to show it. Dozens of illustrations, drawings, and graphs are included.

Intercultural Communication for Business
Elizabeth A. Tuleja

6 Managerial Communication Series | Editor: James S. O'Rourke, IV

ISBN: **0-324-15258-2**

This text examines the basis for culture, reviewing the work of social scientists, cultural anthropologists, and global managers on this emerging topic. Definitions of culture, issues of cultural change and how cultures adapt are included, along with practical examples, case studies, and illustrations of how cultural issues are managed both domestically and internationally.

Listening and Responding
Sandra D. Collins

7 Managerial Communication Series | Editor: James S. O'Rourke, IV

ISBN: **0-324-30167-7**

This text explores how successful companies and effective managers use listening as a strategic communication tool at all levels of the organization. Examples of how organizations have used listening techniques to resolve conflicts, build relationships with clients and employees, and adapt to maintain a competitive edge are discussed.

Writing and Presenting a Business Plan
Carolyn A. Boulger

8 Managerial Communication Series | Editor: James S. O'Rourke, IV

ISBN: **0-324-30168-5**

This text reviews the entire process of writing and presenting a business plan. From idea generation to feasibility analysis, and from writing the plan to presenting it to various audience groups, this text covers all steps necessary to develop and start a business. It also offers guidance on meeting with investors and getting funding for the new venture, and provides numerous samples of effective plans and presentations.

FOREWORD

In recent years, for a variety of reasons, communication has grown increasingly complex. The issues that seemed so straightforward and so simple not long ago are now somehow different and more complicated. Has the process changed? Have the elements of communication or the barriers to success been altered? What is different now? Why has this all become more difficult?

Several issues are at work here, not the least of which is pacing. Information, images, events, and human activity all move at a much faster pace than they did just a decade ago. Among the more popular, hip new business magazines in the past five years is *Fast Company*. Readers are reminded that it is not just a matter of tempo, but a new way of living we are experiencing.

Technology has changed things as well. We are now able to communicate with almost anyone, almost anywhere, 24/7, with very little effort and very little professional assistance. It is all possible because of cellular telephone technology, digital imaging, the Internet, fiber optics, global positioning satellites, teleconferencing codecs, high-speed data processing, online data storage and . . . well, the list goes on and on. What is new this morning will be old hat by lunch.

Culture has intervened in our lives in some important ways. Very few parts of the world are inaccessible anymore. Other people's beliefs, practices, perspectives, and possessions are as familiar to us as our own. And many of us are only now coming to grips with the ideas that our own beliefs are not shared by everyone and that culture is hardly value-neutral.

For a thousand reasons, we have become more emotionally accessible and vulnerable than ever before. You may blame Oprah or Dr. Phil for public outpouring of emotions, but they are not really the cause—they are simply another venue for joy, rage, or grief. The spectacle of thousands of people in London mourning the death of Diana, Princess of Wales, took many of us in the United States by surprise. By the time the World Trade Center towers came down in a terrorist attack, few of us had tears left to give. Who could not be moved by images of those firefighters, laboring in the night, hoping against hope to find a soul still alive in the rubble?

The nature of the world in which we live—one that is wired, connected, mobile, fast paced, iconically visual, and far less driven by logic—has changed in some not-so-subtle ways in recent days. The organizations that employ us and the businesses that depend on our skills now recognize that communication is at the center of what it means to be successful and at the heart of what it means to be human.

To operate profitably means that business must now conduct itself in responsible ways, keenly attuned to the needs and interests of its stakeholders. And, more than ever, the communication skills and capabilities we bring to the workplace are essential to our success, both at the individual and at the societal level.

So, what does that mean to you as a prospective manager or executive-in-training? For one thing, it means that communication will involve more than simple writing, speaking, and listening skills. It will involve new contexts, new applications, and new technologies. Much of what will affect the balance of your lives has yet to be invented. But when it is, you will have to learn to live with it and make it work on your behalf.

The book you have just opened is the seventh of a series of eight that will help you to do all of those things and more. It is direct, simple, and compact. The aim of my Notre Dame colleague, Professor Sandra Collins, is not to provide you with a broad-based education in either business or communication, but rather to pinpoint the issues and ideas most closely associated with the process of *Listening and Responding*. Her approach draws on the latest findings in behavioral psychology and demonstrates why listening may be among the most important yet underdeveloped skills we possess. Becoming an active listener, tuning in to the emotional as well as the cognitive content of what we hear, and learning to provide timely, targeted, and meaningful responses may be among the most important things we can do for our customers, employees, colleagues, and shareholders and others we deal with in the workplace each day.

In the first volume in this series, Professor Bonnie Yarbrough of the University of North Carolina–Greensboro examines issues related to *Leading Groups and Teams*. She reviews the latest research on small group and team interaction and offers practical advice on project management, intra-team conflict, and improving results.

Next, Professor Carolyn Boulger of Notre Dame explores *e-Technology and the Fourth Economy*. With the help of renowned Swedish communication consultant Hans V. A. Johnsson, she looks at the emergence of a fundamental revolution in how people work, live, and earn a living, and she examines how the new technologies have influenced and transformed everything from commercial relationships to distance learning and more.

Professor Collins, the author of this book and a social psychologist by training, has also written *Communication in a Virtual Organization,* the third volume in this series. The conceptual framework she brings to that discussion will help you to understand how time and distance compression have altered work habits and collaboration. With the help of corporate communication executives and consultants, she documents exciting, current examples of global companies and local groups that illustrate the ways in which our work and lives have permanently changed.

For the iconically challenged (those who think in words and phrases, not pictures), Notre Dame professor Robert Sedlack Jr., Northwestern University professor Barbara Shwom, and communication consultant Karl Keller examine *Graphics and Visual Communication for Managers* in volume four of this series. If you have ever wondered how to transform words and numbers into pictures, they can help. And for all of us who have ever tried to explain complex issues without success, either aloud or on paper, the message is simple: if you cannot say it in a clear, compelling way, perhaps you can show them.

Professor Collins is also the author of the fifth volume in this series, *Managing Conflict and Workplace Relationships*. Her approach involves far more than dispute resolution or determining how limited resources can be allocated equitably among people who think they all deserve more. She shows us how to manage our own emotions, as well as those of others. Creative conflict, organizational harmony, and synchronicity in the workplace are issues that too many of us have avoided simply because we did not understand them or did not know what to say.

In volume six, Professor Elizabeth Tuleja of the Wharton School at the University of Pennsylvania examines *International and Intercultural Communication,* looking both broadly and specifically at issues and opportunities that will seem increasingly important as the business world shrinks and grows more interdependent. As time zones blur and fewer restrictions are imposed on the global movement of capital, raw materials, finished goods, and human labor, people will cling fiercely to the ways in which they were enculturated as youngsters. Culture will become a defining characteristic not only of peoples and nations, but of organizations and industries.

Finally, Professor Boulger explores the process of communication and entrepreneurship in *Writing and Presenting a Business Plan*. In a step-by-step approach, she takes us from good ideas ("remember, an idea is *not* a business; it is just an idea") through feasibility analysis to a fully developed business plan. She explains how to identify and influence sources of funding for a new venture, how to package your ideas for the marketplace, and how to present your plan to a venture capitalist. Detailed formats and a sample business plan are included.

This is an interesting, exciting, and highly practical series of books. They are small, of course, not intended to be comprehensive texts, but supplemental readings or stand-alone volumes for modular courses or seminars. They are engaging because they have been written by people who are smart, passionate about what they do, and more than happy to share what they know. And I have been happy to edit the series, first, because these authors are all friends and colleagues whom I know and have come to trust, and second, because this is really interesting stuff. Read on. There is a lot to learn here, new horizons to explore, and new ways to think about human communication.

James S. O'Rourke, IV
The Eugene D. Fanning Center
Mendoza College of Business
University of Notre Dame
Notre Dame, Indiana

INTRODUCTION

The desire to be heard and have our opinions validated is a basic human characteristic. The people who make us feel heard usually capture our support and enthusiasm, whether they are business leaders, political leaders, or pop culture icons. The ability of our leaders to hear our needs and respond to those needs determines if, or how passionately, we follow.

Listening is perhaps one of the most crucial skills that leaders possess. A leader's ability to hear the concerns of customers, employees, and stakeholders determines the organization's success. By hearing and accurately responding to stakeholder concerns, leaders build confidence in the organization and create a culture that builds loyalty and goodwill. By communicating the organization's core values and goals, leaders create a clear message about the organization that stakeholders hear and respond to in a positive way.

Throughout our careers, we lead in different ways. The less seniority we have, the more we listen to others. The more seniority we have in our organizations, the more others listen to us. No matter where we are in our career progression, one element is consistent throughout our development as leaders: our success is determined by our ability to motivate others. We can best motivate by listening to what our stakeholders need and then responding to those needs. We succeed by responding. We know how to respond by listening.

In whatever capacity you lead, you lead better by listening more effectively. By using active and empathic listening techniques, you establish both rapport and trust with your stakeholders, which leads to honest communication. A culture of being heard ensures that your stakeholders speak their minds and alert you to potential opportunities and dangers that may exist. Open communication enables you as a leader to fully understand a situation and then respond and take action that represents the needs of your stakeholders.

Professor Collins presents information that enables us to lead our organizations more successfully. However, her ideas also help us communicate more effectively one-on-one, whether with employees or loved ones. Her suggestions for empathic listening and reflective techniques enable us to build and enhance relationships. By listening, we can improve our employees' productivity and our organizations' bottom line. By listening, we can strengthen the bond between ourselves and those we love.

Professor Collins's background in both psychology and business provides a valuable perspective on the role that listening plays for leaders. She understands how our personal experiences affect our capacity to listen and hear, and she then provides techniques to improve our listening abilities. Professor Collins details how the skill of listening functions within a business organization and provides practical suggestions for leaders to listen more effectively. Her experiences as a psychologist, a business consultant, and a professor at Notre Dame's Mendoza College of Business combine to create a powerful perspective on the most effective ways to listen and make stakeholders feel heard.

The proliferation of electronic communication has increased the amount of information we send and receive. But it has not increased our ability to listen. In fact, it may detract from listening by distracting. Listening has always been a challenge, and it is perhaps more so in this new millennium in which we receive information at a dizzying pace.

More than ever, business needs good listeners: stakeholders need to be heard. This textbook provides practical suggestions that enable you to become a better listener and help your stakeholders feel heard.

Listen, hear, and lead responsively.

Molly Epstein
Director of Management Communication
Goizueta Business School
Emory University
Atlanta, Georgia

CHAPTER

1 LISTENING

This book is designed to give business professionals and students preparing for a career in business a useful tool for improving their listening skills and for achieving organizational goals through listening. To maximize the usefulness of listening as a communication tool for managers, the concept of effective listening is developed at two levels:

- **The listening manager.** We explore listening at the interpersonal level. We look at the process of listening, the goals individuals can accomplish through listening, common listening barriers, and ways to overcome those barriers.
- **The listening organization.** We also introduce effective listening at the organizational level. We discuss the importance of listening well both externally and internally, the organizational goals that can be achieved through listening, and the challenges of creating a listening culture.

This text is organized into four chapters. In Chapter 1, we argue the importance of listening for both managers and organizations as well as the need for training in listening. We describe the listening process and define effective listening for both individual managers and organizations. In Chapter 2, we discuss listening at the interpersonal level, barriers to listening well, and strategies for overcoming them. In Chapter 3, we examine strategies for improving listening in special situations, situations in which a manager may have one of several particular listening objectives in mind. And in Chapter 4, we discuss the listening organization, strategies for achieving organizational goals through listening, and the art of creating a listening culture.

WHY A BOOK ON LISTENING?

Without doubt, each of us is fully aware of the importance of speaking and writing well for success in business. Workshops, articles, and books on public speaking and business writing are ubiquitous. And while the importance of speaking for success in the business world goes without saying (no pun intended), the need for training in listening skills is frequently overlooked. In fact, few business schools offer any courses in listening. Former Chrysler CEO Lee Iacocca summed up the situation when he wrote, "I only wish I could find an institute that teaches people how to listen. After all, a good manager needs to listen at least as much as he needs to talk."[1]

This void in training is especially surprising when we consider how much time we devote to listening at work. According to the U.S. Department of Labor, "The average worker spends 8.4 percent of his or her communication time at work writing, 13.3 percent reading, 23.0 percent speaking and 55.0 percent listening."[2] (See Figure 1.1.) Managers spend even more of their communication time listening—about 60 percent—and executives may spend as much as 75 percent.[3] This means that organizations are spending millions of human resource dollars compensating managers for the time they spend listening, and simply assuming (or hoping) that it's money well spent.

Here's the real problem: In general, people tend to actually "get" only about 50 percent of what is said to them and retain only about 25 percent after 48 hours.[4] Research conducted through WorkKeys—a system of addressing the gap between the skills required by jobs in the United States and the skills offered by employees—revealed a significant gap in the level of listening skills that workers possess and the level demanded by their jobs. More than 20,000 workers participated in a comprehensive listening assessment between 2002 and 2003, and most were found to have skills well below the levels required by their current positions.[5] Listening, in fact, is cited as the communication skill most lacking in new employees. In addition, managers repeatedly say it is the one skill that *other* managers don't do so well.[6] In a survey of *Fortune* 500 companies, 64 percent of the managers were viewed as lacking sufficient training in listening.[7]

It's not that managers don't understand the importance of listening well. Research shows that midlevel managers tend to rate listening as the most frequently used communication skill and the one most important for their professional development.[8] In a survey of 1,400 chief information officers in the United States, 27 percent said that good interpersonal skills were the most important in reaching management levels in the field of information technology. In another study that asked managers to rank skills in order of importance for their success, listening was ranked number one.[9] Yet despite the fact that research confirms people can improve their listening ability with training, few managers ever receive any formal instruction in listening.[10] In one

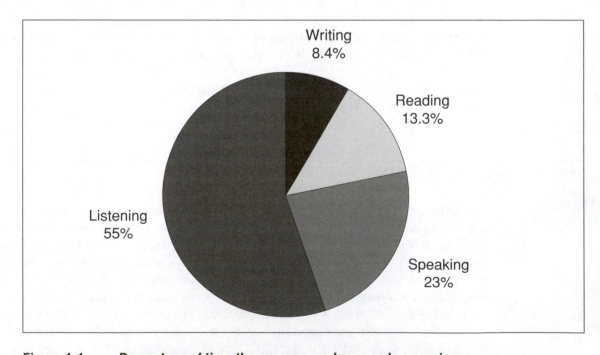

**Figure 1.1   Percentage of time the average worker spends on various
                    communication activities**

recent study, listening was the skill that managers reported wishing they had been taught in college, but weren't.[11]

Three things are clear: Managers spend a great deal of time listening, some don't do it very well, and many could improve their managerial outcomes if they improved their listening skills. So why, with the obvious need, is so little training available? Why do so few business schools offer courses in listening? Two considerations may help answer this question.

- **People fail to recognize the power of listening.** In a results-oriented culture, people are less motivated to engage in activities that don't appear to accomplish a goal. People often fail to recognize the power that a listener holds in an interaction and the potential for accomplishing communication objectives and organizational goals through listening.
- **Listening is not adequately defined.** Listening is a difficult and sometimes frustrating topic to research and write about. Most people agree that it's important, yet in the world of research and academic writing, listening is not clearly defined or well understood. There is some disagreement about what should and should not be included as part of the listening process, how *effective listening* should be defined, and what the preferred general approach to the topic should be. As a result, listening lacks a clear definition, a guiding theoretical framework for research, and a cohesive body of literature from which to derive teaching materials.

In this book, we seek to address these issues by detailing the goals that can be accomplished through strategic listening practices employed by managers and organizations. Furthermore, we offer up a functional and pragmatic approach to defining *effective listening* for individuals and organizations that is based on whether or not the desired outcomes have been achieved through the listening process.

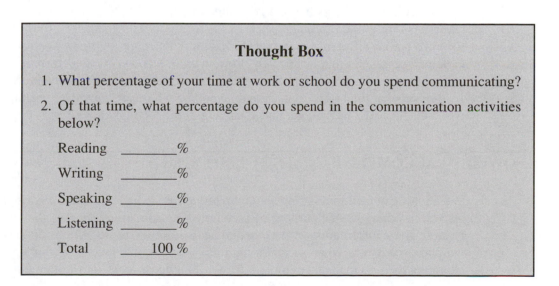

Thought Box

1. What percentage of your time at work or school do you spend communicating?

2. Of that time, what percentage do you spend in the communication activities below?

   Reading   _____%

   Writing   _____%

   Speaking _____%

   Listening _____%

   Total   ____100_%

FAILING TO HARNESS THE POWER OF LISTENING

Why do we fail to recognize the power that a listener holds? Our attitudes and beliefs reflect what we've learned about listening through our observations and experiences, and those attitudes and beliefs are, in turn, reflected in the way we listen. To some extent, the way we listen and our view of listening is shaped by what we observed when were growing up and what was reflected back to us by important others in our social environments. For example, you may have observed a power difference between your parents. Perhaps you viewed your father as the more powerful figure and frequently observed him *not* listening to your mother. Conversely, you may have observed your mother, as the weaker person in the relationship, listening intently to every word from your father. Or perhaps you observed a reversal of those roles.

If we observe more powerful people speaking and not listening and less powerful people listening and not speaking, we might develop the attitude that those in power should do the speaking and those without power should do the listening. When you were a child, in a relatively powerless role, your interactions with adults may have supported this view. If you were told, "Children should be seen and not heard," the general message is that the more powerful party gets to talk and the less powerful party has to listen.

As a child moving through the socialization process, your experiences with various social institutions would have helped shape your attitudes toward listening. In your family, you may have been given messages by your parents that would seem to encourage good listening skills, such as, "Look at me when I'm talking to you," or "Don't interrupt me when I'm speaking." However, these messages are often scolding and create a negative emotional association. The role of listening is treated almost like a punishment. In school or church, we spend most of our time listening while the more powerful, respected, or authoritative figure does all the talking. While this experience can help us learn to be still and listen, if courteous listening isn't modeled back to us when we are speaking, the idea is reinforced that the listener's role is less important.

When we enter the adult world of work, we take these attitudes with us. Employees often complain that managers do all the talking. Employees have ideas, problems, or solutions but aren't able to get a word in edgewise with some managers. Other common complaints employees make about the listening habits of managers are that they interrupt frequently and are preoccupied with other things like the telephone or papers. However, as you can well imagine, the reverse is rarely true. If employees aren't listening to their managers, they will at least act as if they are.[13] The difference is power. In his book *Working with Emotional Intelligence,* Daniel Goleman points out that historically, those with less power are expected to be the better listeners, while those in power feel little obligation to reciprocate. He points to Martin Luther King Jr.'s surprise at the lack of understanding among whites of how black members of society felt, while blacks had a fairly good understanding of the feelings of whites.[14]

THE POWER TO ACCOMPLISH GOALS BY LISTENING

We are accustomed to thinking about the influence we have as speakers or writers. We have all spoken to others for the purpose of accomplishing something, hoping they will comply with a request, share information with us, or perhaps just like us more. When our message is important, we plan in advance what we are going to say, sometimes practicing our statements aloud and changing them to make them more effective. But because we don't often think about the power

---

Thought Box

1. In your family, how do you think power was distributed between the adults in your home? If there was inequity in the distribution of power, did you recall a difference in the time spent speaking and the time spent listening between the two parties? Who was likely to have the "last word?"

2. What was the communication climate in your household when you were growing up? Did you feel like you could talk to your parents about things and they would listen with full attention? Did you feel like they cared about what you had to say? How do you think this may have affected your general feelings of self-worth and feelings about the value of anything you had to say?

3. Do you find situations in your work life where those old feelings may be operating? Do you find yourself not speaking up because you think what you have to say won't be valued?

4. What other institutions contributed to your attitudes toward listening? Were you listened to at school? At church? What messages were you given about listening and the listener's role?

Listen to This ▼

"Who speaks, sows. Who listens, reaps."[15]
—Argentine proverb ▲

we have as listeners, we often overlook the goals we can accomplish through listening. How often have we thought about accomplishing a goal through listening, planned ahead what listening strategies we would use, or rehearsed our listening until we were sure we were ready for an important interaction? This is a much less likely scenario. It's also a missed opportunity.

MANAGERIAL GOALS

In a business environment, we communicate to accomplish specific business goals. Though most of us don't think about listening as a tool for accomplishing goals, we can achieve a great deal through listening well. What can managers accomplish through listening at the interpersonal level?

- **Learning.** Through listening, we learn. As Michael Purdy, a recognized expert on listening, points out, "Listening is our primary means of growth and intellectual development. We impart knowledge when we speak; we learn when we listen."[16]
- **Problem solving.** An inadequate understanding of the nature of a problem is a common reason for failing to produce a good solution. We have all experienced "helpful" salespeople, counselors, or human resources administrators who were so eager to help us solve our problem that they couldn't take the time to listen to us explain it. Gaining a

clear understanding of a problem is the first way that listening contributes to problem solving. Then, once we understand the problem, listening openly to the ideas of others can help us produce a better solution.

- **Building relationships and demonstrating acceptance of others.** Tom Peters believes that leaders should listen intently, not necessarily with the intent of doing everything customers or employees tell them, but, he explains, "By just showing that you're listening, really listening, you demonstrate the respect that you accord to them." Furthermore, Peters points out the tremendous advantage that good listening affords the manager and the organization in the long run. "Intent, tuned-in listening engenders empathy, creates connectedness, and, ultimately, builds cohesiveness. When the crap hits the fan, as it inevitably will, those are the qualities that will see you through." He advises, "Listen while you can so that you can lead when you must."[17] One of the ways we demonstrate our acceptance of others is by listening to them. If I tune you out, I'm saying that I don't care about *what you're saying*. If I do it regularly, I'm saying I don't care about *you*.

- **Enhancing the self-esteem of others.** When we demonstrate our acceptance of others through nonjudgmental listening, we can have a powerful effect on their lives. Research shows that people who have only one person who will listen to them can have a more positive self-image than those who don't have anyone. In particular, empathic listening has the ability to transform lives. It is a powerful tool that we all possess and a tremendous gift that we can give others. What makes listening so effective is that it is a demonstration of our respect or appreciation for another. We aren't just saying we respect the other person—we're showing it through our behavior.[18]

ORGANIZATIONAL GOALS

Clearly, we can accomplish goals as managers through listening, but which goals can organizations accomplish through listening at the organizational level? The same goals as individuals: learning, solving problems, building relationships, demonstrating acceptance of others, and enhancing self-esteem. Organizations can learn how to stay competitive by listening to what their customers want, and they can learn how to help employees do their jobs better by listening to their suggestions. Organizations can make better decisions and produce better solutions by listening to diverse input when problem solving. Organizations develop better relationships with employees by building trust and helping employees feel valued by listening to them.

Thought Box

1. What are your listening goals? In your personal life, which listening behaviors do you want to improve, or in which relationships do you want to improve your listening?

2. How can you improve your work life through listening?

Listen to This ▼

"The key to success is to get out into the store and listen to what the associates have to say. It's terribly important for everyone to get involved. Our best ideas come from clerks and stockboys."[19]

—Sam Walton
Founder, Wal-Mart ▲

Organizations that want to stay competitive need to listen to their customers and respond to customers' changing demands. Consider the example of Pacific Sunwear, a clothing retailer. PacSun started out like so many other little surf shops, peddling surfboards and wax along the beach in California. Unlike its competitors, though, PacSun wanted to continue serving its customers in the winter, when the beaches are empty and all the shoppers are at the mall. PacSun opened the first mall surf shop in 1981 in Santa Monica Place and grew to 21 mall stores by 1987.

PacSun took the California brands, such as Quiksilver and Billabong, which were also born on the beach, first to the malls and then to the East. There PacSun ran into a little trouble when it realized that the weather is cold in other parts of the country and that surf items have limited appeal. But PacSun and its vendors were quick to respond to the needs of the new customers and introduced long pants and long sleeves on surf and skate brands. In 1993, when PacSun went public, it had 60 stores. Today, PacSun has 859 stores and 76 outlet stores in 50 states and Puerto Rico.[20] To what does PacSun credit its success? PacSun's Web site explains it this way:

How does PacSun succeed when thousands of other clothing companies fail? We listen; and we change. Someone once said to the CEO of PacSun, "You give too much credit to those kids." But everyone at PacSun knows the kids have the answers. We listen to get the trends, the solutions and find out what we're doing right. The rest, of course, is history.[21]

Listening to employees is no less important for an organization. Consider the case of Procter & Gamble. In 2000, P&G's top 15 brands were losing market share, the value of its stock had declined, and the company had gone through some major reorganization. The effect on morale was devastating. When A. G. Lafley became CEO in the summer of 2000, he looked to the P&G marketing group to return the company to growth and profitability, but marketing had been affected by restructuring and wasn't in any position to save the day.[22]

Jim Stengel, the future chief marketing officer, began working with two professors from the University of Cincinnati to restore the marketing strength of P&G. Their initial plan was to develop a training program that would fill the skill gaps in the marketing department. To figure out what the training program should include, they asked senior executives which skills they thought were needed (or were lacking) to rebuild the company's marketing strength. They discovered that everyone had a different idea about what the rebuilding process should entail and which skills ought to be developed. The ideas for rebuilding the marketing group were based on the intuition of the executive rather than on research, and each executive had a different perspective about the best way to go.[23]

To put things back on track in the marketing organization, P&G's leadership clearly needed better information about their employees and about what was and wasn't working, so they began an internal research project, initiating conversations with marketing directors, brand managers, and assistant brand managers. Over the course of six months, the researchers listened to employees' thoughts on what was and was not working. Through these conversations, themes emerged about aspects of the organization that interfered with the employees' ability to be effective and also about where things could be changed.[24]

Hearing what employees have to say, of course, is only the beginning of the process of effective listening. To be genuinely effective, the process requires a response of some sort to what's been heard. Based on what their employees told them, Procter & Gamble executives made commitments to change and have kept them. Those commitments have gone a long way toward restoring trust and confidence in the demoralized marketing department. And the results have been evident, both for the employees and for the organization. Surveys show that employees have increased their level of confidence in the company, and 19 of P&G's top 20 brands are increasing in sales volume.[25]

Listen to This▼

"Conversation: a vocal competition in which the one who is catching his breath is called the listener." [26]
—Anonymous ▲

DEFINING THE LISTENING PROCESS

To fully understand how individual managers and organizations can adopt a strategy to accomplish goals through listening and how the role of a listener can be a powerful one, we'll need to develop several definitions: a basic definition of the communication process, a working definition of the listening process for individuals and organizations, and a definition of effective listening for both.

DEFINING COMMUNICATION

Communication is a process that occurs within a system of interconnected elements. The elements of a communication system include the sender of the message, the receiver of the message, the message itself, the means chosen for delivering the message, and the context in which the communication occurs. The context of communication is both physical and psychological. The physical context is the actual environment in which communication occurs, such as the board room or the golf course. The psychological context or environment refers to the mental framing of the interaction. Examples of psychological context include organizational culture, the history of the relationship between the interacting parties, and even temporary states, such as the tension in an organization that is about to undergo major layoffs.

Various sorts of noise are also part of the system. Noise is anything that disrupts or interferes with the communication process. Noise can be physical or psychological, it can disrupt the communication process at any point, and it can be associated with any element in the system. For example, if you are trying to listen to a presentation and a car alarm is sounding outside a nearby window, making it impossible for you to hear, then you have physical noise that is associated with the physical environment or context. If you are listening to a coworker but are preoccupied with thoughts about a recent quarrel with your boss, the noise is psychological and is a property of you, the listener.

Following are a few examples of listening barriers associated with various elements of the model of communication:

- **Sender:** Person speaks too softly and can't be heard.
- **Message:** Message is confusing and poorly constructed.
- **Context:** Environment is too hot or noisy.

- **Receiver:** Listener is preoccupied.
- **Feedback:** Listener doesn't make eye contact with speaker.

Noise isn't necessarily a property of any single element in the model. It is often the result of some combination of elements. For example, power differences between the sender and the receiver may inhibit open communication, an anxious receiver who is easily distracted may not be able to focus in a room with a flickering light, or a mild misunderstanding could escalate to become a major conflict in a stressful environment.

As we are all well aware, noise can and does enter the communication process with annoying frequency. Osmo Wiio, a Scandinavian expert, offers these maxims to help communicators manage their expectations:[27]

- If communication can fail, it will.
- If a message can be understood in different ways, it will be understood in the way that does the most harm.
- There is always someone who knows better than you what you meant by your message.
- The more communication there is, the more difficult it is for communication to succeed.

Two aspects of our definition of the communication process are important to keep in mind for our continuing development of the concept of strategic listening. First, the definition makes clear the equal responsibility of the speaker and the listener for the success of any interaction. Second is the recognition that communication is a system. As such, a change that affects one element in the system will have an impact on the entire system. For example, if you have lunch with a coworker and are in a good mood, your lunchtime conversation will be different than it would be if you were angry and upset. Strategic communication requires considering how all the elements in the process can be used to help accomplish communication objectives and goals. For instance, if you as a speaker want to sell an idea, you might think about how the receiver of your message is likely to respond to your idea and then construct your message in a way that highlights the aspects of your idea that this particular receiver will find most appealing. Strategic listening, then, is simply influencing elements in the model that are under the control of the listener in order to accomplish listening objectives.

Although having a communication goal and planning how to achieve it may be a familiar process for speakers or writers, it may be something we haven't considered as listeners. However, if we are able to achieve the outcomes of learning, or problem solving, or developing relationships through listening, we should be able to plan a listening strategy that maximizes our chances of achieving those goals. A listening strategy involves influencing the elements in the communication system in ways that improve the likelihood that we will achieve our listening objective.

Of course, we have varying levels of control over the different elements in the system. As listeners, we can certainly control our own listening behavior and the feedback we offer the speaker. We may influence aspects of the message through asking questions. And we may be able to have some control over the context of the communication. For example, if we know we listen better in the morning than in the afternoon and in a quiet office rather than a noisy cubicle, we might request that an interaction take place at a certain time (9:00 a.m.) or in a certain location (our office) to enhance our ability to listen.

Listen to This ▼

"Easy listening exists only on the radio."[28]
—David Barkan
International Listening Association ▲

DEFINING LISTENING

The International Listening Association provides a definition of listening that works well to describe the process at the interpersonal level. According to its definition, listening is "the process of receiving, constructing meaning from, and responding to spoken and/or nonverbal messages."[29] Michael Purdy offers a slightly expanded definition that includes memory: Listening is the active and dynamic process of attending, perceiving, interpreting, remembering, and responding to the expressed (verbal and nonverbal) needs, concerns, and information offered by other human beings.[30]

Most current literature on listening breaks down the process into a series of five steps:

1. **Step one is sensing, or the physical processing of sounds selected from the environment.** Most of the time, we are bombarded with more sounds than we could pay attention to, even if we wanted to attend to them all. When we are focused on a task, we may tune out all extraneous noises. To listen to something, we much first select the sounds out of the environment and take them in through our senses. But, of course, listening is more than just hearing sounds.

2. **The second step is interpreting the sounds or assigning meaning to them.** Words, as we know, have no inherent meaning. There is nothing about a dog that makes the word *dog* describe a dog. The meaning of words is subject to interpretation, and interpretations are highly individualized. The meaning we assign to what we hear depends on numerous aspects of ourselves, including our education, our upbringing, and our culture. Even temporary influences, such as our mood, our expectations, or the environment have an impact on the meanings we assign. For example, if you hear a weather siren on the first Thursday morning of the month, you may interpret it to be the regular testing of the warning system. If it sounds on a Wednesday afternoon in the middle of May when the skies are stormy, you may interpret the siren as a warning that a tornado has been spotted. Understanding that our interpretation of messages is highly individualized is particularly important when considering the process of listening to spoken messages.

3. **The third step in the process is evaluating the message.** At this point, we are deciding whether or not we agree with or believe the speaker. We are often unaware that we are engaging in this evaluative step unless we are listening to something we don't agree with or that doesn't ring true. In those moments, we may put a great deal of mental energy into the process of evaluation. Alternatively, we may make up our mind about the message before the speaker has finished and tune out or cut off the speaker. When we don't agree with something we've heard or expect to hear, we may stop listening and start thinking about what we're going to say when it's our turn to speak.

4. **The fourth step in the process is responding.** Our response to a message is the action we take—or don't take—as a result of hearing it. We can respond in ways that let the speaker know the message has been heard and correctly understood. Our response can further an interaction and encourage a speaker. Alternatively, we can respond in ways that directly or indirectly let the speaker know we don't want to listen.

5. **A final step in the listening process is remembering what we've heard.** This is often not considered part of listening, but there is little value to a message that we forget, and, unfortunately, we tend to forget much of what we hear. Information may stay in our short-term memory while we are actively thinking about it and then be transferred to long-term storage, or it may be lost.

So does this definition of listening change when we refer to organizations rather than individuals? Not as much as you might think. In its broadest and perhaps most useful sense for organizations, listening is the process of receiving information and responding to it. It involves the same steps of attending, interpreting, evaluating, responding, and remembering. Organizations that are open to input, that actively seek information, and, importantly, that respond to what is received are listening well.

Though the process is largely similar to interpersonal listening, a few important differences in the way we think about listening at the organizational level should be noted:

- **Sources of information.** Organizations have two broad message resource categories to listen to: internal sources (communication occurring within the organization) and external sources (communication occurring between the organization and an outside entity). Internally, organizations have the opportunity to listen their employees, consultants, and board. Externally, organizations can receive input from their customers, clients, suppliers, investors, local communities, the media, and others.

- **Information seeking**. Organizations need to pay attention to a variety of information from both their internal and external sources. Those sources, however, may not be directing their messages purposely toward the organization. For that reason, organizations may need to actively encourage listening opportunities. For example, employees may be hesitant to pass some information up the organizational hierarchy, and dissatisfied customers may simply go to a competitor without explaining why.

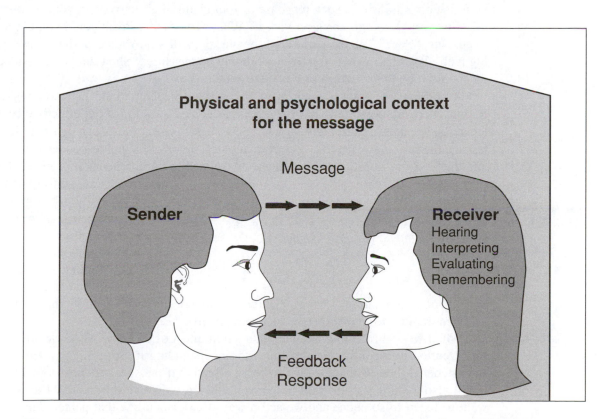

Figure 1.2   The listening process as part of the broader process of communication

- **Processing and managing information.** As with individuals, attending to messages is only the first step in the listening process for organizations. After information has been taken into the organization, what happens next is critical. Listening well at the organizational level requires storing and distributing information in ways that allow the organization to maximize the usefulness of the information with an eye toward improving efficiency, responsiveness, and competitive advantage.

In addition to these differences in how we conceptualize listening at the organizational level, we should also note the social nature of organizational listening. The process of organizational listening is a collective task, requiring coordination, direction, and collaboration across departments and functional areas. This type of effort is best accomplished through a culture of listening, which will mean buy-in from the participants in the organization.

DEFINING EFFECTIVE LISTENING FOR INDIVIDUALS AND ORGANIZATIONS

So, are you a good listener? Most of us think we're pretty good listeners, especially when we're *trying*. But the apparent simplicity of the question is deceptive for two reasons. First, it assumes an understood definition of what it means to be a good listener, and this definition is far from certain. Second, it assumes a valid way of measuring listening effectiveness, which is also not clear cut. What if you think you are a great listener, but your business partner, with whom you communicate more than anyone else, thinks your listening skills leave a lot to be desired? Are you a good listener just because *you* think you are? What if you and your partner argued about your listening abilities, and in response to your claim of effectiveness, your partner said, "Prove it." How would you go about proving it? What sort of assessment could you use and then point to and say, "See?" This scenario begs the questions of who should define what effective listening really is and how that effectiveness should be measured. Should it be the listener's opinion? Or should it be the speaker's? Or is there another way?

According to Sheila Bentley, who writes about benchmarking listening behaviors, at least four answers are possible to the "who gets to decide" question about effective listening: the listener, the speaker, a third party, or a test. Two basic types of tests can be used: the performance test and the pen-and-paper test. A performance test involves having respondents listen to a message and then answer questions about it, usually related to comprehension or recall. Pen-and-paper tests are self-report measures that typically ask respondents to indicate their level of agreement with statements about listening behaviors. Although these types of tests are limited in how well they can assess what actually happens in real-life communication or what a person actually does in an interaction, they can be useful tools for encouraging reflection on one's listening habits.[32]

Listen to This ▼

"Effective listening is engaged listening."[31]
—Tom Peters ▲

When we're in the middle of an interaction, most of us know when we are effectively paying attention to incoming information and understanding it. So it might seem obvious to have the listener decide. But are we really being effective if the speaker doesn't feel listened to? We might also assume that the best judge would be an objective third party. But what if we don't want to listen to someone and we act in ways that discourage that person from speaking (e.g., ignoring a pushy salesperson). If we succeed in shutting down the interaction, which is our goal, are we listening effectively or ineffectively? We've accomplished our goal but have used behaviors that would normally be characterized as poor listening habits. At that moment, for that interaction, a third party may not be a good judge.[33]

The listener, the speaker, a third party, and a test may each be looking at different factors to evaluate listening effectiveness. And, because listening is a process, they may also be making their evaluations at differing points in the process.[34] So the answer to the question, "Who should evaluate effectiveness?" is "None of the above." From the strategic listener's perspective, the criteria used to determine effectiveness should be based on the listener's goals.

For the purposes of this book, it makes sense to define effective listening as the degree to which we achieve our *managerial goals* and *organizational objectives* through listening. Listening is a tactic that leaders and organizations can employ to accomplish objectives. As with any other tactic, we judge it to be effective if we are successful at achieving the outcomes we desire.

Listen to This▼

"A mark of having truly heard someone else is to respond appropriately, even if that means making some change in what you do. But just how far we should go in adjusting our actions based on what another says is itself a matter of some controversy."[35]

—Daniel Goleman
Psychologist and author ▲

Thought Box

1. How well do you listen in different situations? We all listen more or less well in different situations and with different speakers. Evaluate yourself in terms of how well you *usually* listen to the following speakers.

   a. **My boss**
      Very well   Fairly well   Sometimes well/sometimes not so well   Not well

   b. **My mother or father**
      Very well   Fairly well   Sometimes well/sometimes not so well   Not well

   c. **A lecturer**
      Very well   Fairly well   Sometimes well/sometimes not so well   Not well

   d. **My coworker or classmate, whom I hardly know**
      Very well   Fairly well   Sometimes well/sometimes not so well   Not well

   e. **My best friend**
      Very well   Fairly well   Sometimes well/sometimes not so well   Not well

   f. **My significant other**
      Very well   Fairly well   Sometimes well/sometimes not so well   Not well

2. If you found that you listen more effectively with some speakers than others, what do you think contributes to that difference?

LEVELS OF LISTENING

Awareness of our listening goal before we begin an interaction will allow us to determine the appropriate level of listening. Listening occurs at different levels, some more demanding than others. Not all interactions require us to listen at the deepest, most demanding levels. Listening depth or intensity can be conceptualized in a number of ways. Eric Van Slyke, in his book *Listening to Conflict,* posits six levels of listening.[36]

- **Level 1. Passive listening.** This is the lowest level of listening. At this level, we are aware that someone is speaking but actually comprehend little of what is said. We pay little attention and catch only a few words here and there.
- **Level 2. Responsive listening.** At this level of listening, we give the speaker verbal or nonverbal indicators that we are listening, such a head nod or an "uh-huh," but we actually aren't paying much attention, and our comprehension level is still low.
- **Level 3. Selective listening.** When we listen selectively, we are paying more attention to what is said, particularly to words or phrases of some interest to us. We aren't interested in the speaker's entire message, only the part of it that concerns us.
- **Level 4. Attentive listening.** While listening attentively, we may ask probing questions and seek further information from the speaker. We engage our intellect in the listening process and comprehend more information than at previous levels. We are still listening for our own purposes, however, and are probing for more information because the information has some value to us, not because we want to benefit the speaker with our understanding.
- **Level 5. Active listening.** Active listening has become a familiar phrase to many people since its first use in the 1960s. Active listening techniques require listeners to engage not only their intellect in listening, but their emotions as well. Listeners attempt to understand the content of what the speaker is saying, the emotions behind the content, and the conclusions the speaker is drawing but not stating explicitly. Active listeners ask questions to clarify their understanding. They reflect their interpretations of what's been said back to the speaker so that the speaker feels heard and has a chance to correct any misunderstanding.

Reflecting does not mean repeating exactly what has been said. Suppose a coworker comes to you and says, "I can't handle being on both the Cooper and Anderson teams. Both of the project managers act like their project is the only one I'm on. I've just about had it."

What you *don't* want to say as an active listener is, "So what you're saying is that you can't handle being on both the Cooper and Anderson teams. Both of the project managers act like their project is the only one you're on and you've about had it."

This type of parroting exactly what was said is not what is meant by active listening. What's more, it's unnatural sounding to the speaker, and it's annoying.

An active listener might start with a clarifying question, such as, "Are you starting to get overwhelmed?" or "Do you think they're giving you more than you can get done?" This question can lead to clarification and a little more information: "Yeah, I'm drowning in work and I don't feel like I can say anything to either of them, because they're both on the promotion committee."

At this point, reflecting back might be a good idea. The content (I'm overworked) has already been reflected back in the earlier question. Now is an opportune time to reflect back the emotion the person is sharing. "That *is* a tight spot. It's clearly stressing you out."

- **Level 6. Empathic listening.** Empathic listening is listening at its deepest level. It differs from active listening in an important way. When we listen empathically, we try to step out of our own perspective and view things from the other person's perspective, not only understanding what the person is saying and feeling, but empathizing with it. Empathic listening requires listening nonjudgmentally. We cannot empathize with others if we are judging them. Nonjudgmental listening does not mean that we agree with or condone what a person is saying, only that we are willing to step out of ourselves long enough to see how the person views what he or she is saying.

Listen to This ▼

"In empathic listening, you listen with your ears, but you also, and more importantly, listen with your eyes and with your heart. You listen for feeling, for meaning. You listen for behavior. You use your right brain as well as your left. You sense, you intuit, you feel." [37]
—Stephen R. Covey ▲

When trying to improve their listening skills, people often jump to the conclusion that they should listen at the deepest level all the time. But listening deeply is a demanding and draining task. Deep-level listening requires five things:

1. **Motivation.** To expend the energy required for deep listening, we have to be motivated. Being aware of the goals we hope to accomplish through listening can help motivate us.
2. **Ability.** If we are not able to understand a language or technical information, or if loud noise drowns out the speaker, we may not be able to listen to a message, no matter how motivated we are.
3. **Technique.** In addition to raw ability, we need some skill. We need to know how to ask good questions and reflect back the content of message to check our perceptions and let the speaker know that he or she has been understood. This isn't the way we usually communicate, and it takes some practice to make this sound natural.
4. **Commitment.** Listening deeply is not easy. It is not something you will likely be able to do the first time or every time you try it. Developing the ability to listen deeply is a process that takes time. You have to be committed to the process, even within a single interaction. During a lengthy interaction, it is tempting to start thinking about what you want to say instead of listening. You must recommit yourself to your listening task when you find yourself drifting from it.
5. **A listening attitude.** Successful listening at any level depends in large part on the attitude of the listener. This is especially true for deep listening because of the open, nonjudgmental attitude it requires.

Rather than making the decision to listen deeply all the time, strategic listening means that the appropriate level of listening will depend on our listening goals. Basically, strategic listening suggests the following:

- **Different listening goals require different levels of listening.** If we are engaged in purposeful listening, we should listen at the level that will allow us to achieve our objectives.

> **Thought Box**
>
> 1. Has anyone ever told you that you were not a good listener or expressed dissatisfaction with your listening in an interaction? Who was it, and what were the circumstances?
>
> 2. In the situation above, would you agree that your listening was poor, or do you think you listened at an adequate level for your goals in the interaction?

- **Listening goals are determined by considering the entire communication system.** For example, you might consider the importance of a relationship or its expected duration when deciding the appropriate level of listening. Deep listening often requires more investment than is reasonable for a relatively unimportant or temporary relationship.
- **Our ability to achieve our listening goals is determined by the communication system (of which we as listeners are a part).** As we have noted, noise can affect listening at any point in the process and can be associated with any of the elements in the system or some combination of them.
- **Elements in the communication system can be influenced to maximize the likelihood of achieving listening goals.** For example, you can close the door to keep noise in the hall from being a distraction. You can bring water to a meeting so that you won't be distracted by thirst. You can ask a speaker to speak more slowly so that you can better understand a message.
- **Listeners, as elements in the system, can change their listening behavior and have an impact on the entire system.** For example, listening nondefensively to an angry speaker can calm the speaker and change the nature of the message being sent.

In this chapter, we have explored the advantages of listening well and the goals that individual managers and organizations can accomplish through listening. We have introduced the idea of listening at the organizational level and defined the listening process for both organizations and individuals. We have offered a functional definition of effective listening that serves for both individual managers and organizations. We have described the elements in the communi-

> **Guide for the Listening Manager**
>
> Use the following questions to help you prepare for success in a given listening opportunity:
>
> - What is my listening goal for this interaction?
>
> - What is the appropriate level of listening that will accomplish my goal?
>
> - How can I influence the communication system to improve the likelihood that I will accomplish my goal?

cation system and introduced the idea of creating a listening strategy to help us achieve managerial and organizational goals through listening.

In the following chapter we will discuss common barriers to listening well and ways to overcome them. This discussion generally assumes that we are interested in listening at a deeper level, but we should not lose sight of the idea of making listening strategic, which means listening at the appropriate level for our objective.

DISCUSSION QUESTIONS

1. What are the characteristics of a good listener?

2. Do listening skills become more important as a person climbs the organizational ladder?

3. What are your experiences with organizations that you would classify as poor listening organizations?

4. What are your experiences with organizations that you would classify as good listening organizations?

5. How does your culture view the role of the listener in terms of power and importance? Do you think this view varies across cultures?

6. Think of some of the more successful and well-known business leaders of the past decade. Is there evidence that they had good listening skills?

7. To really learn about yourself as a listener, it is helpful to evaluate your listening skills, which you may do with the following self-assessment. However, our own perceptions of how well we listen can be biased. To get a fuller picture of yourself as a listener, complete the self-assessment and then have others evaluate your listening skills using the assessment for others to complete.

SELF-ASSESSMENT

Please rate your level of agreement with each statement in terms of how well it describes you.

1. I usually listen to openly to what others have to say whether I agree with it or not.
   Almost always   Usually   Sometimes   Rarely   Almost never

2. I remember what others have talked about.
   Almost always   Usually   Sometimes   Rarely   Almost never

3. My nonverbal communication tells others that I'm really interested in what they're saying.
   Almost always   Usually   Sometimes   Rarely   Almost never

4. I provide speakers with feedback that lets them know I've heard and understood them.
   Almost always   Usually   Sometimes   Rarely   Almost never

5. I listen well, even when I'm under stress.
   Almost always   Usually   Sometimes   Rarely   Almost never

6. I encourage others to express their opinions.
   Almost always   Usually   Sometimes   Rarely   Almost never

7. In a one-on-one conversation, I usually give speakers my undivided attention.
    Almost always   Usually   Sometimes   Rarely   Almost never

8. I let others speak without interrupting or finishing sentences for them.
    Almost always   Usually   Sometimes   Rarely   Almost never

9. I make sure I don't do too much of the talking when others are trying to communicate with me.
    Almost always   Usually   Sometimes   Rarely   Almost never

10. I am usually open to listening to different sides of an issue before making up my mind.

    Almost always   Usually   Sometimes   Rarely   Almost never

11. I believe other people feel listened to by me.
    Almost always   Usually   Sometimes   Rarely   Almost never

ASSESSMENT OF YOUR LISTENING SKILLS FOR ANOTHER TO COMPLETE

Many people find it useful to make photocopies of this assessment and have it completed by different people with whom they have different types of relationships.

Listening Assessment for _____

1. Do I usually listen to all you have to say, whether I agree with it or not?
    Almost always   Usually   Sometimes   Rarely   Almost never

2. Do I almost always remember what we've talked about?
    Almost always   Usually   Sometimes   Rarely   Almost never

3. Does my nonverbal communication tell you that I'm really interested in what you're saying?
    Almost always   Usually   Sometimes   Rarely   Almost never

4. Do I typically give you feedback that lets you know that you've been understood?
    Almost always   Usually   Sometimes   Rarely   Almost never

5. Do I listen well when I'm under stress?
    Almost always   Usually   Sometimes   Rarely   Almost never

6. When you speak to me, do you feel encouraged to express your opinions?
    Almost always   Usually   Sometimes   Rarely   Almost never

7. Do you usually feel like you have my undivided attention when you're speaking to me?
    Almost always   Usually   Sometimes   Rarely   Almost never

8. Do I almost always let you finish speaking before I say something?
    Almost always   Usually   Sometimes   Rarely   Almost never

9. When you are trying to talk to me, do I tend to do more of the talking than I should?
    Almost always   Usually   Sometimes   Rarely   Almost never

10. Am I usually open to listening to different sides of an issue before making up my mind?
    Almost always   Usually   Sometimes   Rarely   Almost never

11. When you speak to me, do you usually feel that I am listening to you?

| Almost always | Usually | Sometimes | Rarely | Almost never |

12. On a scale of 1 to 10, with 10 being excellent, how would you rate my general listening skills?

| 1 | 2 | 3 | 4 | 5 | 6 | 7 | 8 | 9 | 10 |
| Poor | | | | Average | | | | | Excellent |

ENDNOTES

1. L. Iacocca and W. Novak, *Iacocca: An Autobiography* (New York: Bantam, 1984).
2. U.S. Department of Labor, *Skills and New Economy* (Washington, DC: U.S. Government Printing Office, 1991): 12.
3. M. Purdy, "The Listener Wins." Retrieved Feb. 24, 2004, from http://featuredreports.monster.com/listen/overview.
4. R. Nichols, "Listening Is Good Business." Speech given at the Industrial College of the Armed Forces, August 28, 1964. Publication number L65-13. Transcript available at http://www.ndu.edu/library/ic4/L65-013.pdf.
5. ACT, Inc. Retrieved July 28, 2004, from http://www.act.org/workkeys/assess/listen/index.html.
6. J. E. Meister and N. L. Reinsch, "Communication Training in Manufacturing Firms," *Journal of Business Communication* 25 (1978): 49–67.
7. G. Morgan, "Therapeutic Listening," *Training and Development Journal,* August (1983): 44–46.
8. J. Brown, "Managerial Listening and Career Development in the Hospitality Industry," *Journal of the International Listening Association* 8 (1994): 31–49.
9. Morgan, *supra* n. 7.
10. R. G. Nichols and L. A. Stevens, *Are You Listening?* (New York: McGraw-Hill, 1957).
11. V. Di Salvo, D. C. Larsen, and W. J. Seiler, "Communication Skills Needed by Persons in Business Organizations," *Communication Education* 25 (1976): 269–275.
12. T. Peters, "Rule #3: Leadership Is Confusing as Hell," *Fast Company* (March 2001): 140.
13. P. L. Hunsaker and A. J. Alessandra, *The Art of Managing People* (New York: Simon & Schuster, 1980).
14. D. Goleman, *Working with Emotional Intelligence* (New York: Bantam, 1998), 144.
15. "Listening Quotes." Retrieved Feb. 21, 2004, from *HighGain,* http://www.highgain.com/html/listening_quotes_2.html.
16. M. Purdy, "What Is Listening?" in M. Purdy and D. Borisoff (eds.), *Listening in Everyday Life,* 2nd ed. (Lanham, MD: University Press of America, 1997).
17. Peters, *supra* n. 12.
18. C. R. Rogers and R. E. Farson, "Active Listening," in R. G. Newman, M. A. Danziger, M. M. Cohen (eds.), *Communicating in Business Today* (Boston: D. C. Heath & Company, 1987). Available at http://www.go-get.org/pdf/Rogers_Farson.pdf.
19. "Listening Quotes," *supra* n. 15.
20. "Company Information." Retrieved August 15, 2003, from http://shop.pacsun.com/webapp/wcs/stores/servlet/PSCompany?storeId=10001&catalogId=10001&langId=-1&identifier=ABOUT_US-COMPANY&doc=index.jsp.
21. Ibid.
22. J. R. Stengel, A. L. Dixon, and C. T. Allen, "Listening Begins at Home," *Harvard Business Review* (November 2003): 106–115.
23. Ibid.

24. Ibid.
25. Ibid.
26. "More Quotations About Listening." Retrieved June 15, 2004, from International Listening Association, http://www.listen.org.
27. O. Wiio, "Wiio's Laws—and Some Others," Welin-Göös, Espoo, Finland: 1978. From Steven A. Beebe, Susan J. Beebe, and Mark V. Redmond, *Interpersonal Communication* (Boston: Allyn and Bacon, 1998), 23.
28. "Listening Quotes," *supra* n. 15.
29. International Listening Association, *supra* n. 26.
30. M. Purdy, "What Is Listening?" in M. Purdy and D. Borisoff (eds.), *Listening in Everyday Life*, 2nd ed. (Lanham, MD: University Press of America, 1997), 8.
31. T. Peters, *Thriving on Chaos* (New York: Perennial, 1988), 528.
32. S. Bentley, "Benchmarking Listening Behaviors: Is Effective Listening What the Speaker Says It Is?" *International Journal of Listening* 11 (1997): 51–68.
33. Ibid.
34. Ibid.
35. D. Goleman, *Working with Emotional Intelligence* (New York: Bantam, 1998), 141.
36. E. Van Slyke, *Listening to Conflict* (New York: AMACON, 1999).
37. S. R. Covey, *The Seven Habits of Highly Effective People* (New York: Simon & Schuster, 1990), 241.

2 LISTENING BARRIERS

Speaking to someone who has great listening skills can be immensely satisfying. Speaking to someone who has poor listening skills, on the other hand, can be frustrating and leave us feeling disconnected and discontent. Many poor listening habits are fairly common and quite obvious to the speaker. The International Listening Association has developed a list of the 10 most irritating listening habits.[1] If you were to make a list of your own, it would probably look similar to theirs. Their list includes:

1. Interrupting the speaker
2. Not looking at the speaker
3. Rushing the speaker
4. Showing interest in something else
5. Finishing the speaker's thoughts
6. Not responding to requests
7. Saying, "Yes, but . . ."
8. Topping the speaker's story
9. Forgetting what was talked about
10. Asking too many questions

Most of these irritating habits result from one of two underlying causes. The first is listeners who are focused on their own agenda and what they want to say rather than on the speaker. When listeners are thinking about their turn to talk rather than thinking about the speaker's concerns, they tend to do things such as interrupt, rush the speaker, finish the speaker's thoughts, and top the speaker's story. The second cause of poor listening habits is simply a listener who isn't paying attention.

Many factors can affect how well we listen (see Figure 2.1). In this chapter, we examine common barriers to effective listening. In the previous chapter, we introduced the term *noise* to describe anything that disrupts the communication process. We said that noise can be physical or psychological and can become a disruption at any point in the communication process. Listening barriers are forms of noise that interfere with a listener's ability to listen well or listen at the level necessary to achieve a listening goal. In our exploration of listening barriers, we will focus on those that the listener has the most ability to control. Our discussion of barriers is arranged along the sequence of the listening process: paying attention, interpreting what is said, giving feedback, and remembering.

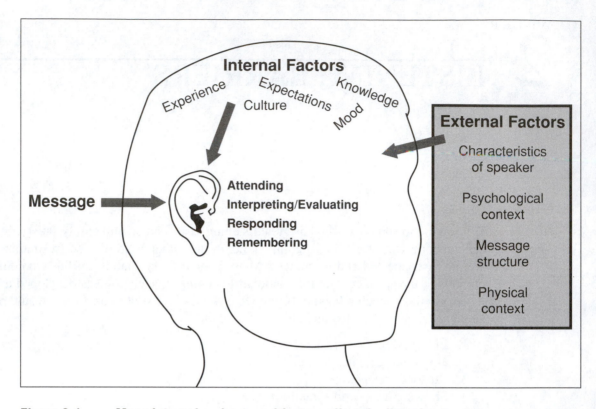

Figure 2.1   Many internal and external factors affect the listening process

Although the discussion in this chapter focuses on barriers over which you as a listener have the greatest control, as a listening manager you are encouraged to consider all the elements in the communication system that you may be able to strategically influence to increase the likelihood of accomplishing your listening objective. For example, you may have some control over context barriers. You may be able to request that a conversation take place at a certain time, or you might be able to control distracting noises by closing a door or turning down a radio. On the other hand, if you are meeting in your boss's office, the environment may be beyond your control. Many aspects of the psychological environment will be beyond your control, as well, but others can be affected by how you communicate. For example, if you are a person of higher status in an organization, that status difference is a part of the psychological environment, which you can't change. You can minimize its impact, however, by being an open and receptive listener.

BARRIERS TO PAYING ATTENTION

The main reason listeners fail to pay attention to a speaker is that they are paying attention to something else. Sometimes their attention is focused inward on themselves, and sometimes it is focused outward. In either case, the listener's attention is focused on something other than the speaker's message.

SELF-FOCUS BARRIERS TO ATTENTION

Part of the psychological context of any interaction is the relationship of the speaker and the listener. Listeners and speakers may feel comfortable or uncomfortable around each other, and to varying degrees. Personality traits, such as shyness or a poor self-image, can lead people to have a self-conscious, uncomfortable attitude when interacting with others. This self-focus can detract from the attention paid to a speaker's message. For example, shy people tend to be more self-focused and experience more negative thoughts during an interaction. Research shows that shy people in a brief conversation with a stranger are more likely to be focused on themselves and experience anxious thoughts during the conversation than people who aren't shy.[2]

But everyone can have moments of feeling uncomfortable and self-conscious when interacting with another. We may find a particular coworker intimidating or imposing, and we may uncomfortable about ourselves when conversing with that person. Or we may have experienced a time when, for whatever reason, we weren't feeling like ourselves, and every interaction was a struggle. Even temporary states can affect our self-focus and how we feel about ourselves. A recent study by Marianne LaFrance, a Yale psychologist, showed that even a "bad hair day" can have a negative effect on self-esteem.[3] Conversely, we have probably also been around people who didn't feel good about themselves when speaking with us. Their nervousness or fidgeting may have given away their lack of self-confidence and also made it apparent that they weren't really listening.

Whether a person's self-focus is a trait or psychological state, paying attention to oneself can impede one's ability to pay attention to listening. Research shows that after an interaction, socially anxious people have a more difficult time remembering information about the other person's appearance and the content of the conversation.[4] When socially anxious people think that another person in an interaction is evaluating them, they tend to avoid looking at the person's face, thereby missing the nonverbal cues of facial expression and eye behavior, which are often critical to truly understanding a message, especially its emotional content.[5]

Focusing our attention on ourselves rather than on what we're listening to isn't always about low self-esteem or "bad hair." Thinking about what we want to say next or how to change the topic of a conversation to one that we want to speak on are also examples of self-focus. Rick, an MBA student from China, was interviewing with an American electronics company. As the interviewer began to explain the company's plans to expand into China, Rick became so excited with what he wanted to say that he interrupted the interviewer. Rick excitedly explained his familiarity with the industry in his country and his ability to help in the expansion but suddenly

---

Thought Box

1. What situations or people make you self-conscious? Think of a recent interaction when you did not feel confident. What led to your feelings? How did they affect the interaction?

2. Is there a particular individual with whom you regularly feel "not okay"? What do you think contributes to this feeling? What could you do to improve how you feel when interacting with this person?

became silent when he noticed the unpleasant facial expression of the interviewer. At that point, the interviewer said, "Rick, please let me finish my words." Rick left the interview convinced he had made a terrible impression.

We have all focused on what we wanted to say from time to time. In a heated debate, we don't want to forget that great counterargument we just thought of or the terrific point we want to make. However, we can't listen well if we are planning what to say when it's our turn to talk. This turns a conversation into a competition and impedes any opportunity for real understanding. In casual exchanges, it might feel like fun and friendly banter, but when the conversation is of a more serious nature, it can be a problem.

LISTENING ENERGY AND ATTENTION

We may plan to get extra sleep the night before we give an important presentation. We may think about the value of being well rested if we have to write a critical proposal. But we *don't* often think about the energy required to listen well. Listening is often thought of as a passive activity that doesn't require much energy on our part. Nothing could be further from the truth. Think about how many times you've dozed off in midsentence or fallen asleep while writing a memo. It is far more likely that we will become drowsy and have difficulty staying awake when we are listening. Whether we're attending a staff meeting or a lecture, we are better able to pay attention and stay engaged when we are well rested.

Being well rested means getting enough sleep, and recent research suggests we probably aren't. Sleep deprivation is a national problem. Surveys conducted by the National Sleep Foundation have found that 60 percent of adults report having sleep problems a few nights a week or more and more than 40 percent of adults experience daytime sleepiness severe enough to interfere with their daily activities at least a few days each month.[6]

The consequences of sleep debt are familiar to many of us. Everyday, millions of people fight to stay alert at home, in school, on the road, and at work. Our sleep debt and the resulting inattentiveness can cause us to make mistakes in every aspect of our lives.[7] Scientists studying sleep debt have demonstrated with magnetic resonance imaging (MRI) of the human brain that sleep debt decreases the entire brain's ability to function. The areas most significantly affected are those responsible for attention, complex planning, complex mental operations, and judgment. Furthermore, the brain doesn't recover from sleep debt after only one good night's sleep, as had been previously believed.[8]

The amount of sleep a person needs to be well rested varies across individuals. Most people need at least eight hours of sleep per night, and some need as much as 10 hours. David Dinges, Chief of the Division of Sleep and Chronobiology in the Psychiatry Department of the University of Pennsylvania, estimates that only 10 percent of Americans can regularly sleep fewer than eight hours per night without harming their health.[9]

Sleep debt isn't the only way to lose your listening energy. Various physical, psychological, and environmental factors can deplete your energy stores as well. For example, if you are ill or experiencing stress, or even if you are just hungry, you may have little

Listen to This ▼

"If you're bored and you're awake, you're just bored. If you're bored and you fall asleep, you've got a sleep debt."[10]

—David Dinges, M.D.
   Chief, Division of Sleep and Chronobiology,
   Psychiatry Department, University of Pennsylvania ▲

energy or patience for listening. If your environment is chaotic or full of conflict, or if it over-loads your senses, your energy for listening can be compromised.[11]

Even certain people can be a drain on our listening energy. Some people can regularly leave us feeling fatigued and negative. Barbara Lau, a freelance writer on communication issues and regular contributor to *Management Quarterly,* calls them "chaindumpers" and is certain that almost every office has one. "If you notice yourself feeling pessimistic, irritated, or fatigued after most encounters with a certain person, then you have one on your hands, too." She recommends limiting the time you spend with chaindumpers and politely interrupting them when they start to unload all their woes. We wouldn't ordinarily think of interrupting another person as a way of listening effectively, and indeed most of this chapter is focused on barriers to listening deeply. But remember that effective listening is defined by whether or not you reach your listening goals, which, in a work context, are determined by organizational objectives. Allowing a coworker to drain your energy through complaints and negativity is not doing anything positive for the organization, and it will reduce your ability to listen when you really need to.[12]

Regardless of what you're listening to, the act of listening itself uses your listening energy. If you are listening to people all day long at work or at school, you may find you have little interest in listening to people when you get home in the evening. You may experience what is called listening burnout. The amount of listening that can be done before burnout occurs varies from person to person. People with introverted personalities tend to run out of listening energy a little sooner than extroverted people because social interaction in general is more energy draining for introverts.[13]

Thought Box

1. How high is your listening energy? During what time of day is your energy level usually its highest? At what point in the day is it at its lowest?

2. What saps your listening energy? What can you do about it? In some cases, you may be able to avoid situations or people that sap your listening energy, but in other cases, you can't. List your energy sappers below and determine how you can minimize their impact by reducing the loss of listening energy or refueling afterward.

Energy Drain	Solution (How can you avoid or reduce it?)
People whom I find draining:	
Internal experiences that I find draining:	
Environmental factors that drain me:	

OTHER ATTENTION PROBLEMS

When it comes to paying attention to a speaker, it doesn't help that people are able to think and listen so much faster than others can talk. People can speak about 140 to 180 words per minute, but people can listen to up to 400 words per minute. What we do with that lag time can make the difference in where our attention goes. If we allow our thoughts to wander, they may wander away from what we're listening to—and they may not ever wander back. If we are listening to a lecture, we may begin daydreaming and may not quit until the lecture is over.

So we might ask what would happen if we didn't have that lag time. In a set of studies, speech was compressed to fit more speech into less time. However, rather than just speeding up the speech, like pressing a "fast-forward" button that makes speakers sound like squeaky mice, advanced technology was used to compress the speech in such a way that it maintained its normal sound and clarity. Evidence from these studies suggests that people may retain more if they engage in "fast listening." The thinking is that more brain power is engaged when listening to accelerated messages. According to Joel Galbraith, a researcher at Penn State University, "If you're listening at accelerated speeds, it forces you to *not* do anything else, so you're more focused on it."[14]

Another familiar problem with listener attention is competing stimuli. Distractions in the environment can make paying attention difficult. Often, we have no control over these distractions. Anyone who has ever worked in an office cubicle and tried to listen to someone on the phone while a conversation took place in the neighboring cubicle knows that it can be tough to pay attention in those circumstances. But sometimes we invite the competing stimuli. In this fast-paced world where everyone is under pressure to work harder and faster and get more done in less time, it's not surprising that we find ourselves multitasking.

Think of all the many things we attempt to do while listening. Or, better yet, think of all the listening we try to do while we're doing other things. Unfortunately, we all have a limited amount of mental capacity available to us at any given moment, and managing more than one task at a time means splitting our mental capacity between them. In some cases, this might be fine. Perhaps we can sort mail or reorganize our desktop while we talk on the phone. But what if the task is more mentally demanding? Can we really listen on the phone and, say, respond to e-mail? As Marcel Just, codirector of Carnegie Mellon University's Center for Cognitive Brain Imaging, says, "It doesn't mean that you can't do several things at the same time, but we're kidding ourselves if we think we can do so without cost."[15]

Of course, in some listening situations, the cost of multitasking has little to do with the limits of our mental capacity. Not all interactions are only about getting the information right. Sometimes the most important goal of an interaction is how the speaker feels about it, that the speaker feels worth our time and attention. You may easily be able to read the paper while listening to a coworker describe what he did on his vacation and not miss a single word he says. But will your coworker feel listened to? Will he feel satisfied with the interaction, even if you do get all the information right?

One final difficulty with paying attention is sometimes called "the entertainment syndrome." Kurt Cobain summed this problem up fairly well in the chorus of Nirvana's hit song

---

Listen to This ▼

"You cannot truly listen to someone and do anything else at the same time."[16]
—Scott Peck
Author, *The Road Less Traveled* ▲

> **Thought Box**
>
> **How much does daydreaming affect you?** In some cases, our daydreaming may not cause us any difficulties. Perhaps we are in a situation where we are listening to something that is of no interest to us and of no predictable value. For example, you may accompany a friend to a lecture on a topic that you find boring. You have gone along only to provide companionship to your friend, so you daydream during the presentation. The cost to you is minimal. You won't be able to discuss your take on the lecture with your friend, but that may be the only cost you incur. Often, however, we daydream when we are listening to information that may be valuable to us. We daydream through a class and figure that we can read the material in the textbook later. We catch ourselves daydreaming in a meeting and hope that no one asks us a question at that moment. At the very least, daydreaming may not be the best use of our time. Furthermore, it can cause us to miss out on valuable information. To see how much you daydream, choose a formal listening situation with little or no interactivity. Then record the number of times you catch yourself daydreaming. Anytime you monitor your behavior, you are likely to change it in the desired direction. So if you want to daydream less, continue monitoring the amount of daydreaming you do. As you see yourself progress by daydreaming less, be sure to reward your efforts.

"Smells Like Teen Spirit," where the song suggests that young people expect to be entertained.[17] With the technology available today, we have become accustomed to listening to messages accompanied by music soundtracks and special visual effects. It's hardly surprising that a spoken message by a single person, with no light show, backup dancers, or laugh track, can seem a little boring. We can use the lack of luster in a spoken message as an excuse for not listening to it, but we do so at our own peril. Information that is valuable to us will not always be presented in an entertaining way. We should avoid dismissing speakers just because they aren't exciting.[18]

BARRIERS TO INTERPRETATION

One night, two friends agreed to meet after work for a drink at a local TGI Friday's. However, Friday's has two restaurants in their town, and the friends each went to a different location. The next day, they were both a little angry at having been "stood up." As we know, attending to a message is only the beginning of effective listening. Simply getting the information doesn't mean we are getting it right. We still have to interpret what we hear. Miscommunication happens. It's both common and costly. Sometimes the costs are limited to time, a little money, and a measure of frustration. But sometimes the costs are much more substantial. Both the *Challenger* and *Columbia* disasters have been attributed to communication problems within NASA.[19]

Listening barriers that interfere with the correct interpretation of a message are all basically attributable to the same thing: differences among us. If each of us were exactly the same in every way, misunderstandings wouldn't occur. But, because we have different goals, different tastes, different histories, different beliefs, different interests, and so on, we may well have different perceptions of what we hear. Our differences mean that what one person finds interesting to talk about, another person may find boring to listen to; what one person thinks is crystal clear, another person finds as clear as mud, and what one message can mean is something different to everyone who hears it.

Examine the picture in Figure 2.2.[20] Can you tell what it is? This picture does a nice job of illustrating the difference between sensation and perception. Sensation is the process of taking energy in through our senses, whereas perception is the process of interpreting the information. While we are looking at the picture, we all see the same black spots on a white page. As we attempt to make sense out of what we're seeing, some of us interpret it as a picture of a Dalmatian; others may interpret it as something else. How we interpret what we take in through our senses is influenced by a number of things, including, but not limited to, the following:

Figure 2.2   What is it?

- Attitudes
- Values
- Beliefs
- Mood
- Expectations
- Education
- Previous experience
- Background
- Culture

INTERPRETING VERBAL COMMUNICATION

In March 2003, the United States bombed downtown Baghdad in a campaign based on a concept called "Shock and Awe" developed at the National Defense University. American newscasts featured video of the bombs bursting, one after another, and flames lighting the night sky. The words *Shock and Awe* were almost certainly chosen with careful consideration of how they would contribute to the shaping of attitudes toward the tactic. Naming the campaign "Really Intense Bombing" would not have had the same effect. The dramatic video and the "Shock and Awe" label created a frame through which the bombing could be viewed by Americans as a stunning display of the United States' military strength. However, as one student who was living in the Ukraine at the time put it, "Not everyone saw it that way." Other cultures may have viewed the campaign through a different frame and had a very different interpretation.[21]

Words can shape our expectations, interpretation of events, and memories. Carefully chosen words can shape a listener's experiences in several ways:

- **Creating a "frame" with words.** Speakers can shape the responses of a listener by choosing words that create a "frame" for listener's perceptions. Objects, events, and ideas can often be described in multiple ways. Words have denotative, dictionary-type meanings, but they also have connotative meanings that influence their interpretation. For example, inexpensive jewelry is preferable to cheap jewelry, even though both *inexpensive* and *cheap* could refer to the same thing: the low cost of the jewelry. Consider how you might talk about a newly hired coworker who is a recent graduate, fresh out of school. If you like the person, you may frame the situation positively (the person is eager to learn), or you may frame the situation in a more neutral manner (the person is inexperienced) or in a more negative fashion (the person is naïve).

- **Guiding interpretation with preemptive words.** Some words are considered *absolute terms* or *preemptive words* in that they are predicted to elicit a common response in most listeners. Words such as *justice* and *child welfare* will typically create a predictable response. It's hard to imagine anyone being against *justice* or having a negative reaction to *child welfare*. Psychologist Robert Zajonc offers the word *evil* as an example of what he calls preemptive words. He argues that regardless of whether the word is used by the United States when referring to terrorists or by terrorist groups when referring to Americans, the result for anyone who accepts the description is the same. "Evil is a preemptive word. It is preemptive because it imposes on us only one form of understanding, only one meaning." Speakers often recognize the power of preemptive words or absolute terms and use them in an attempt to shape the responses of the listener.[22]

- **Arousing emotions through words.** Words can also create intended or unintended emotional reactions in listeners. Some words are emotional triggers or *hot button* words, which can arouse a serious emotional reaction in the listener. The exact words that are hot buttons vary from person to person. Words that are emotional triggers can engage and arouse listeners in a desired way; however, they can also distract listeners or lead them to shut down their listening. Furthermore, speakers risk losing credibility by using hot button words. Catherine had been working at her new job for a few months when she ran into her boss, Emily, as they were both leaving the office for the day. They took the elevator together and began a casual conversation. Although Catherine's position was fairly autonomous and she didn't know Emily very well, Catherine admired her. She considered Emily to be a consummate professional. Emily had an impressive work history and a flawlessly professional appearance. But as she and Catherine conversed in the elevator, a stream of obscenities started to flow from Emily's mouth. She wasn't angry or being emotional. The conversation was typical elevator talk—except for the swearing. Catherine was taken aback, distracted by the words she was hearing, and unable to think of Emily in quite the same way after that.

- **Reconstructing memories through words.** Words can shape our memories as well as our interpretations. In a study conducted by Elizabeth Loftus, participants were shown a video of two automobiles in a collision. After viewing video of the accident, some participants were asked to estimate how fast the cars were going when they "hit" each other. The rest were asked to estimate how fast the cars were going when they "smashed" into each other. When the estimates of speed were compared, the researchers found that the group that had been asked the "smashed" question gave significantly higher estimates of speed than the group asked the "hit" question. Changing a single word changed how the groups interpreted the event. Furthermore, a short time later, the researchers called these same participants and asked them whether they remembered seeing broken glass in the video. There was no broken glass, but significantly more people from the group given the "smashed" question remembered seeing broken glass than the group given the "hit" question. Both the interpretation and the memory of the event were affected by the change of one word in a question.[23]

"Memory is deceptive because it is colored by today's events."[24]
—Albert Einstein ▲

Words can shape our listening experience and our memories, and, on the other hand, we and everything that contributes to making us who we are can shape the meaning of words. Many words have multiple meanings and can be interpreted differently by different listeners. Furthermore, people are highly likely to use ambiguous words and phrases when they speak. For example, they may say, "Joe works too much," or "Lisa makes a ton of money." But how much work is too much, and what dollar amount constitutes a ton of money? Listeners will interpret ambiguous words and phrases according to their own experience, expectations, and culture. And those interpretations may vary considerably from what the speaker intended. One middle-aged financial expert frequently refers to the women he works with as "the gals in the office." He doesn't mean anything derogatory by it, but to most people it is not interpreted as an empowering term. Using that phrase to refer to the female managers in his office doesn't make the women sound professional or powerful, and they might find it insulting.

The effect of using words such as "gals" is the like that of using more familiar stereotyping words, which most people recognize as being politically incorrect. When we use a stereotype, we label a social group or a member of a social group and apply a collection of beliefs to them. It is important to note that the content of stereotypes is not necessarily negative. For example, we may have a stereotype of CEOs that includes the characteristics *intelligent, energetic,* and *visionary.*

Furthermore, stereotypes can be functional. From a cognitive functioning standpoint, using stereotypes helps us simplify our social worlds. If we create social categories and store a collection of beliefs about each of them, we don't have to start from scratch every time we encounter another person. For example, when we think of the social group "accountant," we probably think "good with numbers." When we meet someone new and learn that he or she is an accountant, we don't wonder about the person's skill with numbers. We simply apply the stereotype.

The main problem with stereotypes is that we apply them indiscriminately to all people in a group, even though all people in the group are not the same. Not all accountants, for example, are good with numbers. Another problem with stereotypes is that they are often associated with prejudice, which is typically defined as a negative attitude toward a particular social group or member of that group.

In one study of this tendency, participants were given information about "Hannah," a nine-year-old girl. Some of the participants were told that Hannah's parents were well-educated professionals and lived in an affluent community. Other participants were told that Hannah's parents were blue-collar workers and that the family lived in a low-income area. The participants were then shown a videotape of Hannah taking an achievement test and were asked to rate her ability. Her performance on the test was actually average, and even though everyone saw the same tape, those who thought she came from a poor background rated her performance significantly lower than did those who thought she came from a more affluent background.[25]

As listeners, when we apply stereotypes or think prejudicially, we shape our expectations of what we will hear from another person. This doesn't mean that we're simply surprised when we hear something we didn't expect. The effect of expectations on listening is far more complex than that. Our expectations will affect our choice of which information we listen to and how we interpret it.

People tend to have a confirmation bias in information gathering, wherein they selectively attend to what they expect.[26] Teri was in the first year of owning a small specialty retail shop. She had financed the venture with her own savings and a small loan. She was confident in her ability to succeed, but her mother thought the whole idea was too risky and was bound to fail. Her mother was adamantly opposed to the entire idea from the start, so they rarely talked about the shop. After nearly a year of operation, Teri's mother asked how the shop was going. Teri told her that things were basically going well, monthly sales had been increasing steadily, but some weeks were better than others. They talked about a few other things, and at the end of their conversation, as they were saying their goodbyes, Teri's mother said, "I'm sorry things aren't going well at the shop."

What's even more interesting is that our expectations about the people we listen to can lead them to behave in ways that confirm our expectations. In one study, male and female participants were put into pairs—without seeing each other—and asked to have a conversation using a phonelike apparatus. The male participants were shown a picture, ostensibly of the female with whom they were interacting. In actuality, the pictures were not of women participating in the study. Half the men were shown a picture of an average-looking woman, and half were shown a picture of an attractive woman. After a brief conversation, the males shown the picture of the attractive female formed a more positive impression of her personality than the men shown the picture of the average-looking woman. In addition, the men shown the attractive picture were perceived to behave in a friendlier manner during the interaction. However, this study yielded an even more surprising result. Later, audiotapes of the interactions were played for independent participants. These listeners were permitted to hear only the female side of the conversations. After hearing the women's side of the phone conversation, these participants rated the women who had been speaking to males shown the attractive photograph as warmer, more confident, and more animated. In essence, the men expecting a more attractive partner created one.[27]

INTERPRETING NONVERBAL CUES

An enormous amount of the meaning of any spoken message is communicated nonverbally. Nonverbal communication serves numerous functions, some of which assist us in our verbal communication, including regulating verbal interactions (we raise our hand when we want to ask a question in class), accenting or "punctuating" our verbal messages (we make an assertive statement and pound the table for added emphasis), or repeating our verbal messages (we hold up two fingers when we say we want to make two points). At times our nonverbal message may substitute for our verbal message (we wave "hi" instead of saying it). In other cases, our nonverbal communication may contradict our verbal message (we yell, "I'm not upset!").

For listeners, nonverbal communication is critical for two reasons: Nonverbal cues help us determine the intended interpretation of a speaker's words, and our own nonverbal cues are a critical means of offering feedback to speakers.

Most nonverbal cues fall into one of the following categories:

- **Vocalics.** Vocalics refers to everything about a spoken message except the words themselves, such as the tone of voice or pace of speech. When we listen to others, we learn a great deal about how they would like us to interpret their words by how they say them. Think of all the many times you've heard your name called and the different ways it has sounded. When you hear your name, you can probably tell fairly easily whether someone is angry with you, pleased to see you, or trying to get your attention.

- **Gestures and posture.** Gestures and postures communicate, sometimes intentionally and sometimes despite our sincere attempt to prevent them from communicating. Gestures that have a clear meaning to a particular group are called *emblems:* A teacher holds a finger to her lips to shush someone speaking too loudly, a hitchhiker puts out a thumb to catch a ride, a college student motions with her finger to ask someone across the room to come toward her. *Illustrators* are movements that help illustrate or make clear the verbal content of a message. If you are describing a smooth, flat surface to someone, you may move your hand from side to side in front of you, as if you were running your hand over the surface. *Regulators* are nonverbal cues that help regulate verbal interaction. In a meeting, we may avert our eyes if we don't want to be asked a question. On the other hand, we may hold up a finger or our pen to indicate that we do want to answer. *Affect displays* communicate our emotions. We can often tell whether someone is feeling happy or sad simply by looking at them. *Adaptors* are nonverbal behaviors that help a person cope with stress or discomfort, such as wringing one's hands or chewing on a pencil.
- **Facial expressions.** Across the globe, facial expressions are the primary means of communicating human emotion. Nonverbal communication is our primary means of communicating our emotions, especially through our facial expressions. Paul Eckman is a psychologist and the world's foremost expert on facial expressions. He has lent his expertise to the Federal Bureau of Investigation, Hollywood filmmakers, and the Dalai Lama. In his research, Eckman found seven primary emotions, communicated through facial expressions, that are universally understood (i.e., anger, sadness, fear, surprise, disgust, contempt, and happiness). People in the highlands of Papua New Guinea, isolated from any exposure to Western culture, were able to recognize various expressions when looking at photographs of Western faces. Furthermore, the New Guinea natives were asked to pose for the camera displaying various expressions, and the expressions in those pictures were easily recognized by people in the West.[28]
- **Eye behavior.** As listeners, we know that, at least in American culture, maintaining good eye contact with speakers is expected. In fact, as you may have noticed, not looking at the speaker holds the number two spot on the International Listening Association's top-10 list of irritating listening habits, given at the beginning of this chapter. Attending to the speaker's eye behavior not only helps the speaker feel listened to, it also helps listeners understand the speaker's message better. Eye behavior can reveal confidence or nervousness, warmth and caring, doubt and fear, or other emotions that add a vital dimension to a message.
- **Appearance.** Appearance includes such things as a person's body shape, skin color, hair color and length, and facial features. Most people are well aware of the dangers of making judgments about a person based on his or her appearance, even though we may find certain aspects of a person's appearance difficult to ignore. On the other hand, some aspects of a person's appearance may provide us with useful information that we don't want to ignore. It may be desirable to attend to certain aspects of appearance, such as age or gender, that may help listeners better understand the speaker.
- **Artifacts.** Artifacts are human-made objects, such as clothing, jewelry, furniture, tools, and art. In organizations, artifacts communicate a great deal. Status differences may be communicated through clothing. Organizational culture can be communicated through furniture or decorations. We use artifacts such as clothing, jewelry, or tattoos when we make judgments about a speaker. If we compare public figures like Matt Lauer and

Steven Tyler, we're likely to make different assumptions about them as people based on the artifacts they present. Most people attend to artifacts more than appearance factors such as eye color or height because people are known to have more control and choice about artifacts than they have about appearance. The concern for us as listeners is that we may form conclusions about the value of a speaker's information or tune out a speaker based on our interpretation of the speaker's artifacts.

- **Space.** The use of space is a nonverbal cue that influences communication in several ways. First, allocations of amounts of space and preferred space can communicate value. The larger offices or the corner office is often given to members higher on an organizational hierarchy. Second, the way a space is arranged will influence the communication that occurs within it. For example, a room with rows of chairs facing front and a podium will encourage a different form of communication than will a room with chairs arranged in a circle. Finally, in an interpersonal interaction, we are affected by the norms of personal space. These norms vary by culture, but within cultures, people have a strong sense of how near or distant individuals in different types of relationships should be from each other when interacting. When speakers violate our personal space, it can be distracting and make it difficult for us to focus on what they are saying. When we observe others communicate, we can make inferences about the nature of their relationship.

- **Time.** The way we use time is a method of communicating nonverbally. As listeners, we communicate our interest in others by our willingness to spend time focusing on them. In addition, the communication of speakers and listeners can be dramatically affected by time urgency. Even when we are very interested in what a person is saying, our ability to demonstrate that interest through our listening can be compromised if we are in a hurry.

Despite the importance of nonverbal cues, they can be difficult to interpret. Nonverbal communication is often ambiguous and requires information about the context to make its meaning clear. A waving hand can have a multitude of meanings. In isolation, the meaning of the wave would be impossible to determine. But nonverbal cues don't occur in isolation; rather, they are multichanneled. A facial expression is accompanied by a gesture and a tone of voice, all of which contribute to the meaning of the message.

As listeners, the richness of any interaction is derived from both the verbal and nonverbal elements. Consider the following story, and note how the conclusions at the end of the interaction rest on its nonverbal aspects.

The other day, I went into a store to exchange a pair of pants for some in a different size. I went to the service counter and stood behind a woman who was returning some bedding. The customer service representative seemed to be annoyed with the woman, and I attributed that to the woman's demanding tone and terse manner. When the woman left, I took my place at the counter and gave the customer service clerk a moment to finish what she was doing and give me her attention. It soon became clear to me, however, that she had no intention of giving me her attention. She was looking down at what she was working on and didn't seem to plan on looking up anytime soon, so I had to start my explanation of why I was there without her even making eye contact—which was very uncomfortable. She glanced up at me while I spoke but didn't maintain eye contact. Instead, she looked back at what she was doing. I was short on time and everything in the store had been moved around, so I asked her if she could

---

Thought Box

1. How do you let a speaker know through your nonverbal communication that you are not interested in what is being said? How do you hide from a speaker the fact that you are not listening?

2. Describe a time when you made a judgment about a person based on the person's appearance or artifacts that you later learned was incorrect. How did your judgment affect your listening?

3. Have you ever been in someone else's room or office where you immediately felt comfortable? What made the room feel that way?

---

point me in the right direction to find the pants I was exchanging. She pointed in a direction—the wrong one, as it turned out—and said, "Over there." I left that store feeling like I had inconvenienced her by coming in. She took care of my exchange, so I know she heard what I said and understood me, but that wasn't enough to make me feel listened to. I could tell she didn't care why I was there or what I had to say—she just wanted me to go away.

CULTURAL DIFFERENCES AND INTERPRETATION

Advanced communication technologies and the ease and affordability of air travel have opened the gateway for the development of a global marketplace. Most of us will experience the need to communicate across cultures at some point in our work lives. This means that intercultural listening will be required of us if we are to succeed in these interactions.

Culture refers to the way things are done in a group. The dimensions of a culture are its language, physical aspects (e.g., art, architecture), and psychological aspects, (e.g., social hierarchies, religious beliefs). Every society has a cultural heritage that includes the traditional beliefs, artifacts, thoughts, and intellectual traditions that are handed down from one generation to the next. As we grow up in a culture, we go through the socialization process of *enculturation,* wherein we learn how to live in our society.[29]

Often the most difficult aspect of intercultural communication is overcoming language barriers. Certainly, people who speak different languages face some obvious challenges in communicating. However, culture can shape the use of language so that people from different cultures, even when they share a common native tongue, may have difficulty speaking and listening to each other. For example, in the United States, *homely* means plain or unattractive. In England, however, *homely* means warm and comfortable.

Informal, conversational language can create problems for people from different cultures. For example, words and phrases that are commonly used in American business culture (e.g., *affect the bottom line, cut through the red tape, run it up the flagpole*) are confusing to people for whom English is a second language, because the words' denotative meanings make no sense. Regional sayings can also create confusion.[30] In the eastern United States, a soft drink is a soda; in the Midwest, it's a pop; and in some parts of the South, it's all called Coke, no matter which brand or flavor it is.

Listen to This ▼

"Having grown up in a traditional Chinese family and also being in Western culture myself, I do see some entrenched habits of interpretation of the world that are different across the cultures, and they do lead to pervasive differences." [31]

—Patricia Cheng
UCLA ▲

Culture shapes communication in profound ways, from the language we use to the topics we discuss. Communicating across cultural differences often means that language and the meaning of nonverbal cues are different between communicators. This is challenging enough, but intercultural communication can be a formidable task for other reasons as well. Most of us don't know a great deal about other cultures; however, we make assumptions about them. Often we assume similarities that don't exist (people would not eat eyeballs). Where we find differences between cultures, we tend to exhibit ethnocentrism, or to view the differences from the perspective of our own culture. In other words, we think of our own culture as being the "right" one (eating eyeballs is disgusting). In addition, we tend to see the characteristics of our own culture and ourselves differently from the way others see us. Americans tend to be informal and direct in their communication, which they view as friendly, straightforward, and open. Some other cultures view American informality and directness as rude and undisciplined. [32]

Listening carefully to popular phrases and words used in conversation can help us learn a great deal about a culture. Examining common sayings can reveal the beliefs, values, and attitudes of a culture. Here are some values of American culture and popular sayings that reflect them. [33]

Value	Saying
Time	"Time is money." "Time is of the essence."
Individualism	"Do your own thing." "He's his own man."
Task Orientation	"Keep your eye on the ball." "Keep your nose to the grindstone."
Self-reliance	"Stand on your own two feet." "Pull yourself up by your bootstraps."
Directness	"Tell it like it is." "Stop beating around the bush."
Materialism	"You can have it all." "He who dies with the most toys, wins."
Competition	"Winning isn't everything, it's the only thing." "If you can't stand the heat, get out of the kitchen."
Informality	"Loosen up." "He's a stuffed shirt."

Cultures also vary in terms of how much a listener must attend to the context of a message to understand it. All communication is affected by the context in which it occurs. As listeners, paying attention to the context of communication can improve our understanding of messages. But the degree to which the meaning of messages actually depends on contextual cues varies by culture. In some cultures, known as high-context cultures, words mean very different things depending on the context. In low-context cultures, the meaning of a message is contained more directly in the words. Chinese, Japanese, and Latin American cultures are examples of high-context cultures. German, Swiss, and American cultures are on the low-context end of the scale. Listeners from high-context cultures have been socialized to attend to implicit meanings in messages and carefully observe nonverbal behavior. They are more likely to respond to their gut-level reaction to what they hear rather than to the facts or statistics presented in a message. People from low-context cultures are more likely to spell things out with explicit, verbal communication, something that could be considered inappropriate and even insulting in a high-context culture.[34]

Recent research suggests that culture shapes not only what we think about, but also *how* we think. Westerners tend to be more analytical in their thinking, while Easterners are more holistic thinkers. Affecting the way we think will, of course, affect the way we communicate. In one study, Japanese and American participants were shown an animated underwater scene of fish and plants and were asked to describe what they saw. Japanese subjects made 70 percent more comments about the background or context than did American participants. American participants were more likely to focus on the biggest or fastest fish or the brightest object. The most surprising finding in this study is that when the same fish was shown with two different backgrounds, the Japanese participants had difficulty recognizing it as the same fish. The researchers interpreted this as evidence that, for the Asian participants, the fish was inextricably tied to the context.[35]

GENDER AND INTERPRETATION

People don't have to be from different cultures to feel as if they're speaking different languages. As noted at the beginning of this chapter, people can interpret things differently, even if they have similar backgrounds. Gender differences in communication style have been of interest for years as men and women have struggled to understand each other. These differences have become of particular interest to members of the business community as more and more women enter the workforce and achieve high-ranking management positions.

Deborah Tannen, a professor of communication and author on the topic of differences between male and female communication styles, has written about a number of common differences in the way men and women communicate at work. She points out that conversation is often ritualized, meaning that many of our conversations follow an understood pattern. According to Tannen, "We say things that seem the thing to say, without thinking of the literal meaning of our words any more than we expect the question 'How are you?' to call forth a detailed account of aches and pains."[37]

Conversation rituals are not a problem when everyone speaking

Listen to This▼

"Our brain findings on listening do not mean that either men or women do it better or worse, they just appear to do it differently."[36]

—Michael Phillips
Indiana University School of Medicine ▲

is following the same ritual or when differences are expected. Sometimes, we anticipate rituals to be different and possibly even confusing, such as greeting rituals in a foreign country. "But we don't expect differences," says Tannen, "and are far less likely to recognize the ritual nature of our conversations, among other Americans at work."[38] Often, men and women have different rituals for conversation. For example, women tend to apologize ritually. Women often apologize in conversations not because they are sorry for something they've done, but rather because they are expressing empathy with the person speaking. So, for instance, a woman listening to a person talk about encountering difficulties getting to work, such as being pushed on the subway or getting splashed on the street, might respond with an, "I'm sorry." Clearly, the woman isn't at fault, but she offers a ritual apology. Men, on the other hand, don't typically apologize ritually.

Women and men differ in the degree of directness in their communication. Both men and women are direct at times and indirect at others, but the situations in which they use direct and indirect communication vary. Women tend to be less direct when they are giving orders. Orders from a woman often sound like suggestions. For example, rather than saying, "Put it over there," a woman manager might say, "We could put it there," or "It might look good there."[39] In an episode of *The Apprentice* with Donald Trump, a team had been whittled down to two members, a man and a woman. In a segment of video, the woman, Amy, is shown talking to the camera while she is away from the man, Nick. She says that she thinks Nick made a mistake by trying to tell an event planner how a room they were trying to lease out should be set up. She felt that telling the event planner how the room should be arranged would stifle the planner's creativity. But when Amy expressed these concerns to Nick, she didn't come right out and say that she wanted him to stop telling the planner how he envisioned things. Rather, she just said (at least in the video the audience was able to see), "Sometimes I think it's better to just shut up and listen."[40] This indirectness is, in part, a result of socialization in which women are taught not to be "bossy" and in which they learn that they can get farther with an indirect method of communication. At work, however, indirect communication may be unclear or may be seen as weak.[41]

Listen to This ▼

"'Neutron Jack' Welch and 'Chainsaw Al' Dunlap may have inspired men, but macho leadership styles continue to alienate women." [42]

—Margaret Heffernan ▲

Differences in the communication styles of men and women frequently involve listening. Women often complain that men don't listen. In fact, a study conducted by Shere Hite, author of *The Hite Report,* found that 77 percent of women surveyed answered the question "What does your partner do that makes you the maddest?" with "He doesn't listen." If the survey had been completed by only a few respondents, we may not have considered this statistic terribly important, but the study included 4,500 female respondents.[43]

There is no evidence that men are simply unable to be good listeners, but there is evidence to support the idea that males and females listen differently. Some of these differences are physical in nature. In a study conducted by Michael Phillips, a neuroaudiologist at the Indiana University School of Medicine, and his colleagues, brain scans revealed differences in brain activity between men and women while listening. The study suggests that men listen with the left side of their brain, and women listen with both brain hemispheres. Phillips is quick to point out that the study doesn't imply that males or females are better listeners, only that their brain activity appears to be different while listening.[44]

Men and women also appear to have differences in their listening style or preference. According to Larry Barker and Kittie Watson, authors of the book *Listen Up,* people use one of four possible listening preferences:[45]

- *People-oriented listeners* are concerned with how listening affects relationships. They are less concerned with the content of a conversation than they are with the fact that the conversation is occurring and that they are able to interact with another person. People-oriented listeners are easily able to connect to the emotional content of a message and may, at times, get swept up in it. They are the kind of people to whom others love to bring their problems because they listen nonjudgmentally. Others can sometimes take advantage them because people-oriented listeners can get caught up in the emotion of others' problems.
- *Action-oriented listeners* are focused on listening to information that will help them accomplish the task at hand. They like to get to the root of things and have little patience for people who ramble on. In a work environment, the fact that they encourage others to stay on topic can be valuable and appreciated.
- *Content-oriented listeners* like to listen to complex information and lots of details. They are evaluative listeners, and they like examining information closely. They prefer to listen to experts. However, they can take a long time to make decisions because they like to analyze all the evidence from every angle.
- *Time-oriented listeners* tend to be focused on the time they have available to listen and may even make a point of mentioning this to the speaker. They are impatient with people who appear to be wasting time and may repeatedly glance at the clock or their watch while listening.

Males tend to be action-oriented listeners, whereas females tend to be people-oriented listeners. According to the authors of *Listen Up,* listening preference isn't about listening ability, and we may demonstrate different listening styles depending on the situation. No doubt, everyone has been a time-oriented listener at some point.[46]

This approach also suggests that different styles of listening would be more effective, as well as preferred, depending on the situation. In a work environment, action-oriented listening might be preferred in a project meeting, content-oriented listening might be best for a discussion of a complex proposal, and people-oriented listening would work best for building relationships.

Some people have difficulty switching from one style of listening to another. In an episode of ABC's *20/20,* a reporter visited Al, a baseball scout, and Linda, his wife, who had different listening preferences. Al was an action-oriented listener and did a lot of his work from home, taking phone calls and viewing baseball tapes. Linda was a people-oriented listener who tried to get Al to listen to her. Al had a difficult time making the transition from action-oriented listening to people-oriented listening when interacting with Linda. He frequently tuned her out to the point of not responding to her questions because he was focused on baseball and she was talking about something else.[47]

Other common differences between the listening behaviors of men and women include the following:[48]

- **Tuning out distractions.** Men tend to be better at tuning out distractions and competing messages than women. In one study, men and women listened to two stories at the same time and were told to pay attention to only one. Then they were asked questions about the content of the stories. The men in the study performed better than the women, who were less able to tune out one story and focus on the other.

- **Questions.** Because women are often people-oriented listeners, they tend to be highly aware of conversation as a way to build relationships. They often consider the act of conversing more important than the actual content of the conversation and may ask questions to simply keep an interaction going. However, men tend to ask and expect fewer questions and can feel as if they are being interrogated when too many questions are asked.

- **Emotions.** Women tend to be a little better than men at interpreting emotions. However, this difference does not hold when women are compared with men trained as counselors and other therapeutic professionals. Those men are equally as skilled as women at interpreting emotions.

- **Interruptions.** Even in early childhood, males tend to interrupt more frequently than females. This tendency doesn't appear to abate with age. Men tend to interrupt more than women, with one notable exception—women who have advanced degrees interrupt more than men.

- **Giving advice.** When men listen to women talk about a difficulty or problem, they want to help them solve it. Women, however, are often seeking only an empathetic ear and can be put off by male advice giving. Diane, a small business owner, was speaking to a male friend about her business. She told him that she had misplaced an important tax document and despite her efforts, she hadn't been able to find it. Her friend responded with, "Well, I wouldn't spend too much time looking for it. Just look for it a little while longer and if you don't find it, write to ask for another copy." A short time later in the conversation, Diane mentioned that a plumbing problem had been repaired in her office building. Originally, the plumber had thought the problem was outside her unit, but it actually turned out to be inside it. She wasn't sure whether that meant she would have to pay for the repair or whether the building owner would still be responsible. Her friend responded with, "I wouldn't say anything to the owner. Just wait to see if she sends you the bill." When the conversation ended, Diane felt dissatisfied and later complained, "It's not like I didn't know what to do in either of those situations. I was just talking about my day. I didn't need anyone to tell me how to handle it."

It's important to note that for each of these general differences, there are men and women who are exceptions. Some men ask a lot of questions, and some women are great at tuning out distractions. Some men avoid giving advice, and some women are looking for advice when they bring up a problem. Generalities of this sort are not meant to suggest that every man or every woman behaves in a particular way, but rather to reveal differences in general tendencies.

Thought Box

1. Do the research findings on gender differences in listening resonate with your experience, or does your personal experience disconfirm them?

2. Think of a time when you communicated with someone from another culture. What were the challenges you encountered?

OTHER DIFFICULTIES WITH INTERPRETATION

The differences among people often lead to differing interpretations, posing a barrier to effective listening. Often, though, the difficulties we experience with interpreting what we hear result from either a lack of mentally processing a message or distortions that occur during processing. We've discussed several important contributors to processing errors already, such as our expectations or intense words. Here are a few additional common examples:

- **Labeling information.** We may choose to simply shut down our processing of certain types of information. Some people choose not to discuss religion; for other people, it's politics; and for still others, it might be labor unions. Many people have at least one topic that they simply choose not to talk about or listen to.
- **Fear of difficult material.** Some people may expect material to be too difficult to understand and may choose to not process it for fear of failing in their attempts. They essentially giving up before trying.[49]
- **Different preferences for information.** We all need information, but we may have different preferences for the depth and complexity of the information we receive. Some people like lots of details and want to hear every available piece of information. Others want "just the facts" or only the necessary information. Speakers and listeners are often mismatched in terms of their preferences, which can lead to one or the other becoming frustrated or bored. In a casual conversation, Kelly asked Jack how many children his office assistant had. Jack replied with the names, ages, and residency of each of his assistant's six grown children. Early on in his answer, Kelly, who expected a single-word answer, tuned out Jack. When Jack started to give the names and ages of the grandchildren, too, Kelly cut him off by saying, "I don't really need to know all that." Both left the interaction feeling frustrated.

MEMORY BARRIERS

Many of us wish that we had better memories, and for good reason. Researchers Ralph Nichols and Leonard Stevens estimate that we retain only about 50 percent of what we hear immediately after we hear it and less than that as time goes by.[50] Memory is the process of encoding, storing, and retrieving information. Most researchers in the area of memory conceptualize memory as different memory systems (i.e., sensory memory, short-term memory, and long-term memory), each with a different specific function.[51]

MEMORY SYSTEMS

When energy is taken in through our senses, it enters our sensory memory. For a brief instant, we have an almost perfect recall of that information. But sensory memories quickly fade, and we lose most of the information we've taken in.[52] Some of the information we take in will go into our short-term memory, also called our working memory. Short-term memory is limited in duration. Information doesn't stay in short-term memory for long once we've stopped working with it. Short-term memory is limited in capacity as well. We are able to hold about seven (plus or minus two) bits of information in our short-term memory. Although that doesn't seem like much, we are able to use a process called chunking to help us hold more information.

    Consider the information given in Figure 2.3 If you look at line 1 for a moment and then look away, you may find it difficult to reproduce the seven figures. But if you look at line 2 for a moment and then look away, you would have very little trouble reproducing it. Similarly, if you compare lines 3 and 4, you would probably agree that line 4 could be remembered more quickly and easily than line 3. And if you look at line 5 for an instant, it would be difficult to remember after looking away, but line 6 would be easy to recall. Why is it easy to recall the contents of line 6 and nearly impossible to remember line 1, when line 6 clearly holds so much more information? The difference is chunking. Chunking is the process of taking pieces of information and combining them into a meaningful unit. For line 1, you have to recall the shape and direction and orientation separately because they can't be organized into a readily recognizable meaningful unit. Line 6, on the other hand, has shapes that can easily be organized as letters, and the letters can be chunked together as words, and the words can be chunked together as a phrase, making it possible to store much more information in short-term memory but count it as only one bit.[53]

Some of the information in our short-term memory is transferred to our long-term memory. This happens in one of two ways: effortful processing or automatic processing. Much of the information that goes into our long-term memory is put there by our efforts. When we want to remember something, we engage in effortful processing, working with information, often through rehearsal, to transfer it to long-term storage. With automatic processing, information enters long-term memory with no conscious effort on our part. An exciting moment, traumatic event, or something we find personally important can enter our long-term memory automatically, whether we want it to or not.[54] At about 11:00 p.m., Connie was stopped at an intersection with her left turn signal blinking, waiting for a break in the oncoming traffic so that she could turn left. She glanced in her rearview mirror just in time to see a car barreling up behind her, not slowing. The car swerved slightly before impact and smashed into the right rear of Connie's car, making a horrible crunching metal sound. Connie's head snapped back, giving her a severe case of whiplash, but there were no other injuries. Shortly after the accident, Connie's car was repaired, and no evidence of the accident remained—except for Connie's memory of seeing the approaching car in her rearview mirror, a memory she experienced every time she was at an intersection turning left and noticed a car coming up behind her.

---

1. ι;θακλβ
2. AGTLNBK

3. HET STBE GNHTI NI FEIL REA EREF
4. THE BEST THINGS IN LIFE ARE FREE

5. THINGS BEST WORM ARE BIRD THE
   EVERY VENTURED FREE A NOTHING
   IN THE HAS CLOUD EARLY GAINED SILVER
   THE GETS LIFE LINING NOTHING
6. THE BEST THINGS IN LIFE ARE FREE
   THE EARLY BIRD GETS THE WORM
   EVERY CLOUD HAS A SILVER LINING
   NOTHING VENTURED NOTHING GAINED

Figure 2.3   **Chunking helps us hold more information in short-term memory.**

MEMORY FAILURES

We have difficulty remembering for several reasons, including encoding failure, decay, retrieval failure, and interference. To illustrate how each of these types of failure works, we'll use the example of remembering the name of someone you have just met during a job interview.

- **Encoding failure.** Students often express a desire to improve their ability to remember names, but one problem with remembering names is that they sometimes don't make it into memory in the first place. When we meet someone for the first time, especially for a job interview, we might be nervous and concerned about the impression we're making (you never get a second chance to make a first impression). As a result, we may fail to really process the person's name and put it into memory. Repeating the person's name in that initial meeting is a way to guarantee that at least you encoded the name in the first place. Of course, it doesn't guarantee that you will remember the person's name later, but it's a start.[55] In addition to distraction, this sort of encoding failure can be the result of lack of interest. We might not think information is important enough to remember. Think for a moment about the appearance of a penny. A penny has eight design elements. Can you name them? We all have a great deal of experience with pennies, but most of us can't describe what they look like in any detail. This is because we fail to put this information into memory. It is simply not important enough.

- **Decay.** Even a bit of information that has without doubt made it into our long-term memory system may not be retrievable when we want to access it. It is believed that long-term memory is unlimited in capacity and duration. In other words, we never run out of room in our memory, and we don't lose a memory just because it's from our childhood. However, there is a theory that unused information in long-term storage may begin to spontaneously decay over time. In our interview example, this might happen if you interviewed with a number of people years ago, before you found the right job. The names of some of those people with whom you interviewed may be lost from your memory by now.

- **Interference.** Sometimes the information is in our memory, but we can't seem to get it back out. This can happen when one piece of information interferes with another in memory. For our example, let's say you interviewed with several people and one person was named Sarah and another was named Sharon. Later, you may have a hard time remembering Sarah's name because Sharon's name is interfering. This type of interference is more likely when the two pieces of information are similar to each other.

- **Retrieval failure.** At a given moment, we may be completely unable to remember information we are sure we know, only to remember it with ease a while later. When we experience this sort of retrieval failure, we can jog our memory through *priming,* or remembering what we can *around* the memory we're trying to access. For example, imagine you are trying to remember one of your interviewer's names. You said the name a few times when you first met the person, so you know it's in your memory somewhere. To help you remember the name, you

Listen to This ▼

"First you forget names, then you forget faces. Next you forget to pull your zipper up and finally, you forget to pull it down." [56]
—George Burns ▲

could think about the other things you talked about. You could even remember what you were wearing and how you were standing when the person was introduced. All these memories can help you activate the one you're trying to access.[57]

In general, the most effective way to improve your memory is to process information deeply. This means repeating the information frequently, actively thinking about it, and relating the information to what you already know. The more associations you form between new information and information you already hold in memory, the easier it will be for you to retrieve the new information when you want to recall it. For listeners this means that rather than simply listening passively, we should be using the processing lag time to actively think about the information we want to remember.

FEEDBACK AS A LISTENING BARRIER

Responding is a critical step in the listening process that serves both the listener and the speaker in several ways. In many listening situations, the goal of feedback is to clarify the listener's understanding, reflect the listener's interpretation of a message back to the speaker, and communicate the listener's interest in the speaker. Basically, the goal is to further the interaction in the speaker's intended direction. It is through our feedback that the speaker reaps the benefit of our listening. If we listen carefully, but then do not provide the speaker with an adequate response, we haven't listened well.

Feedback can be a hindrance rather than a help to effective listening. We can make feedback errors that shift the direction of an interaction away from the speaker's intended message or that simply end the interaction prematurely. Feedback errors can leave speakers feeling frustrated and dissatisfied. Common feedback errors include the following:

- **Questions.** Questions are an important part of effective feedback. Through questions we are able to get additional information to better understand speakers, check our perception of their message, and let speakers know we are really interested in understanding them. But questions can be leading or even accusing, and those sorts of questions are obviously not helpful to an interaction. Furthermore, asking too many questions can be annoying and make speakers feel as if they are being interrogated.
- **Denial.** When we respond to others by denying what they say, we can shut down an interaction with our feedback. When we say things like "It couldn't have been that bad" or "Oh, come on," or even simply show nonverbal signs of our doubt, we are communicating our disbelief in what the person is saying.
- **Faultfinding.** The last thing most of us want when we are looking for a sympathetic ear is a listener who wants to help us recognize how whatever it is we're complaining about is our own fault—even if it is. At times, as listeners and managers, we may have no choice except to point out a person's mistakes, but as listeners we should ask ourselves what our goal is in doing so. If we are trying to listen supportively, faultfinding is a poor strategy. When we respond with comments such as "He wouldn't have said that to you for no reason" or "Well, what did you think was going to happen?" we are not being supportive.
- **Advice giving.** Again, as listeners and managers it may be our responsibility to give advice. On the other hand, if we are listening with the goal of being supportive or even with the goal of furthering the interaction, advice giving can have the opposite effect.

The behaviors that make feedback effective are dependent on the listener's specific goal. Different listening goals will require different types of feedback. For example, listening with the intent to learn a new procedure might require asking a number of questions about details, taking notes, and repeating the exact words back to the speaker to be sure the procedure is clearly understood. These same behaviors on the part of a listener with the goal of being supportive would be inappropriate.

In very general terms, effective feedback involves the following:

- **Displaying immediacy cues.** Immediacy cues are affirming nonverbal displays. They communicate interest and liking to the speaker. Immediacy cues include leaning in toward the speaker, eye contact, nodding, or smiling.
- **Asking questions.** Although it's true that asking leading or accusatory questions can be a mistake, asking no questions is equally as costly to effective listening.
- **Reflecting content.** By reflecting back the content of a speaker's message, listeners can be sure they are interpreting a message in the manner intended. This can take the form of perception-checking questions (e.g., "So, do you mean . . . ?") or paraphrasing of the speaker's words.
- **Reflecting feelings.** According to Carl Rogers and Richard Farson, "In some instances, the content is far less important than the feeling which underlies it. To catch the full flavor or meaning of the message, one must respond particularly to the feeling component."[58] Understanding how a speaker feels and letting the speaker know that you do may be the most important thing you, as a listener, can do at these times.
- **Reflecting conclusions.** When we listen to others, we draw inferences and conclusions that may go beyond what is actually stated. While this is a necessary part of conversation, we should check any inferences or conclusions we are uncertain about with the speaker. For example, Brandon was an assistant manager at a retail store and was about to leave for the day when a customer came in to return a product she had purchased that had a manufacturer's defect. The product was a special order, and to give the woman a replacement, one had to be ordered and the defective product returned. Brandon told the woman to come back in a week and the replacement product would be there. Before he left, Brandon told the general manager, who was coming on duty, about the situation so that the manager could take over. However, the manager's conclusion from listening to Brandon was that he had placed the order and shipped the defective product already. When the woman returned a week later, Brandon and the manager discovered that neither of them had placed the order.

As listeners, our effective feedback leads to a more successful interaction for the speaker and for us. We gain a better understanding of the speaker's message, let the speaker know our interpretation of the message, and communicate our interest in the speaker and the topic.

SUGGESTIONS FOR OVERCOMING GENERAL LISTENING BARRIERS

The concept of strategic listening suggests that we set a listening goal for ourselves and then influence the elements in the communication system to improve our chances of achieving our goal. Effective listening in various listening situations, such as listening to learn or listening to show support, requires different, specific listening behaviors. However, as we have seen, some behaviors can interrupt our motivation or our ability to listen at deeper levels in general. The following suggestions summarize ways to overcome these general listening barriers.

DETERMINE A LISTENING OBJECTIVE

To be successful in listening situations, we should be clear about what it is we want to achieve and what level of listening is necessary to achieve it.

CONSIDER WHAT MIGHT AFFECT YOUR MOTIVATION AND ABILITY TO LISTEN

Certain aspects of your ability to listen are related to you, and other aspects of your ability are affected by other elements of the communication system, such as the context or the message. Knowing yourself and anticipating the challenges you will face in a given listening situation is a significant step toward effective listening. The following are ideas for achieving your best performance as a listener.

MANAGE YOUR LISTENING ENERGY

Knowing what saps your listening energy can help you plan ahead for important listening situations. You can learn how to manage your listening energy so that you have the energy you need for important listening situations:

- **Get enough sleep.** If you have a difficult interaction coming up, you will be able to deal with the related stress more effectively if you have had enough sleep. In a formal listening situation, such as a lecture, where the opportunity for active participation is limited, it can be hard to stay attentive if you are sleep deprived. Being sleepy can turn even an interesting lecture into a torturous exercise. Sleepy students report biting the inside of their cheek, pinching themselves, and munching on chewable No-Doz in an effort to stay awake through lectures. Even if they manage to stay awake using these techniques, their listening will certainly be subpar. Getting enough sleep is a much more valuable approach.

- **Listen to your circadian rhythm.** Through a course of 24 hours, every person experiences a cycle of various stages of alertness, from sleeping to being fully awake, which is sometimes called our body rhythm. You may think of yourself as a morning person or a night owl. This reflects your understanding of you own body's energy cycle. Throughout the day, we have peaks and valleys in our energy level that are fairly predictable (at least when we are on a somewhat regular schedule). Many people feel a dip in their energy right after lunch or in the midafternoon. Knowing the rhythm of our energy levels enables us to manage our schedules better. If you don't think clearly until noon, or if you are nearly in a coma by 2:00 p.m., plan accordingly. When you can, arrange your schedule around your peak energy levels. When you can't do that, take steps to raise your listening energy: Take a short nap, drink a cup of coffee, or walk briskly around the office a few times.

- **Take time to refuel.** When our listening energy is low or spent, we need time to refuel. We may need to take a break from a heated discussion. We may need to tell our spouse we need 30 minutes to ourselves after we get home from work. Most people would prefer to know that a listener needs a break rather than speaking to someone who isn't really able to listen.

MINIMIZE INTERNAL AND EXTERNAL DISTRACTIONS

Having enough energy to stay focused is important, but for most of us, it's not sufficient to ensure our undivided attention. If possible, we should reduce distractions that will compete for our attention.

- **Minimize internal distractions.** Internal distractions, such as hunger, thirst, or anxiety can take energy and attention away from listening energy. It's easy enough to make a point of eating a light snack before a lecture or be sure a pitcher of water and some glasses are on the conference table before a meeting. Some internal distractions, such as illness or emotional upset, aren't so readily eliminated, but we can attempt to minimize them. Taking a cold pill or pain reliever won't cure us of an illness, but it may help us feel well enough to get through a listening event. Similarly, if we know an interaction is likely to be emotionally upsetting, we can plan for our emotional reaction in advance so that we don't let it get the best of us.
- **Control external distractions.** We don't always have control over our physical context or surroundings, especially at work. But trying to tune out distractions in the environment consumes our energy and reduces the supply available for listening. Turn off the radio, or close the door to your office if you're able to. You can also manage the context for the communication by arranging the room in a way that promotes listening and by making the space for communication comfortable.

HAVE A LISTENING MINDSET

You will perform better as a listener if you prepare yourself mentally for listening. You can prepare for listening in several ways:

- **Develop your curiosity.** A listening mindset results from true curiosity. If you are actually curious about what someone is saying, you will be motivated to listen. In order to be truly curious, you must suspend your judgment. It's hard to listen to something if you've already made up your mind.
- **Evaluate your biases.** Consider what biases or preconceptions you may have about the speaker or topic that may be operating when you are listening. Awareness of biases can help control for or correct for their influence to some degree.
- **Prepare for cultural differences.** If you will be listening across cultures, learning a little about the speaker's culture can help. Recognizing existing differences can help you guard against making erroneous assumptions.

MANAGE THE CONTEXT TO THE EXTENT THAT YOU'RE ABLE

In some cases you will have a great deal more control over the context than in others. It pays to take control over elements in the context that may disrupt your ability to listen where possible.

- **Arrange the room in a way that promotes listening.**
- **Make the space comfortable for communication.**
- **Be sure your have time to listen.** If not, let the speaker know. That's preferable to rushing the speaker.
- **Offer effective nonverbal and verbal feedback.** Remember that the nonverbal elements of your listening will communicate a great deal to the speaker about your interest in him

or her and your openness to what you're hearing. This is corroborated through verbal responding in the form of good questions, reflections back to the speaker of the content and feelings behind the message, and your conclusions.

Becoming a more effective listener is an endeavor that requires motivation and commitment. It is a lengthy process, and even after investing time and effort, you will doubtlessly catch yourself exhibiting listening barriers and walking away from an interaction thinking about how you could have done a better job of listening. We will never be perfect listeners, but with determined effort, we can most certainly become better listeners.

DISCUSSION QUESTIONS

1. Create a list of the 10 listening habits you find most irritating, and compare it with the list from the International Listening Association. What are the differences and commonalities? Make a list of your own worst listening habits, and compare the lists.

2. Some organizations have implemented a napping policy during office hours. Would you recommend this as a way to improve listening among employees?

3. What strategies do you use to help yourself pay attention to a lecture you don't find interesting?

4. When words are heard repeatedly, they can shape beliefs and attitudes. How can managers create organizational climate by carefully choosing and using certain words?

5. Can a room or an office communicate the occupant's willingness to listen to those who enter? How?

6. Imagine you were going to have a meeting with a group of people from another country. What would be a good way to prepare for this meeting?

7. What is the best way to deal with the situation when someone remembers an event or statement differently from the way you remember it, and you're both certain your memory is correct?

ENDNOTES

1. "International Listening Association." Retrieved January 7, 2004, from http://www.listen.org.
2. L. A. Melchor and J. M. Cheek, "Shyness and Anxious Self-Preoccupation During Social Interaction," *Journal of Social Behavior and Personality* 5, no. 2 (1990): 117–130.
3. M. Vilar, "Ever Had a Bad Hair Day?" *Science World* (Sept. 18, 2000).
4. D. A. Hope, R. G. Heimberg, and J. F. Klein, "Social anxiety and the recall of interpersonal information," *Journal of Cognitive Psychotherapy* 4, no. 2 (1990): 185–195.
5. W. Mansell, D. M. Clark, A. Ehlers, and Y.-P. Chen, "Social Anxiety and Attention Away from Emotional Faces," *Cognition and Emotion* 3, no. 6 (1999): 673–690.
6. APA Online, "Importance of Sleep." Available at: http://www.apa.org/pubinfo/sleep.html.
7. National Sleep Foundation, "NSF 2005 Sleep in America Poll." Available at: http://www.sleepfoundation.org/hottopics/index.php?secid=15&id=115.

8. ABC News, March 30, 2002. Available at http://www.abcnews.go.com/sections/2020/2020/2020_010330_sleep.html

9. Ibid.

10. Ibid.

11. L. Barker and K. Watson, *Listen Up* (New York: St. Martin's Press, 2000).

12. B. Lau, "Energy Sappers: There's One in Every Office," *Management Quarterly* 32, no. 3 (Fall 1991): 39.

13. Barker and Watson, *supra* n. 11.

14. D. Heingartner, "Now Hear This, Quickly," *The New York Times* (October 2, 2003): E1, E6.

15. S. Shellenbarger, "Multitasking Makes You Stupid: Studies Show Pitfalls of Doing Too Much at Once," *The Wall Street Journal* (February 27, 2003): D1.

16. "More Quotations About Listening." Retrieved February 13, 2004, from http://www.listen.org/quotations/morequotes.html.

17. K. Cobain, "Smells Like Teen Spirit," *Nevermind.* Geffen Records, September 24, 1991.

18. J. J. Floyd, *Listening: A Practical Approach* (Glenview, IL: Scott, Foresman, 1985).

19. R. Stenger, "Concerns Raised That Changes in NASA Won't Last." Available at http://www.cnn.com/2003/TECH/space/08/26/sprj.colu.shuttle.report/.

20. B. E. Goldstein, *Sensation and Perception* (Belmont, CA: Wadsworth, 1980).

21. "Iraq Faces Massive U.S. Missile Barrage." Available at http://www.cbsnews.com/stories/2003/01/24/eveningnews/main537928.shtml.

22. R. B. Zajonc, "The Preemptive Power of Words," *Dialogue: The Official Newsletter for the Society for Personality and Social Psychology* 181 (2003): 10–13.

23. E. Loftus and J. C. Palmer, "Reconstruction of Automobile Destruction: An Example of the Interaction Between Language and Memory," *Journal of Verbal Learning and Verbal Behavior* 13, no. 5 (1974): 585–589.

24. "Brainquote.com." Retrieved February 24, 2004, from http://www.brainyquote.com/quotes/authors/a/albert_einstein.html.

25. J. Darley and P. Gross, "A Hypothesis-Confirming Bias in Labeling Effects," *Journal of Personality and Social Psychology* 44, no. 1 (1983): 20–33.

26. M. Snyder and W. Swann, "Behavioral Confirmation in Social Interaction: From Social Perception to Social Reality," *Journal of Experimental Social Psychology* 14, no. 2 (1978): 148–162.

27. M. Snyder, E. Tanke, and E. Berscheid. "Social Perception and Interpersonal Behavior: On the Self-Fulfilling Nature of Social Stereotypes," *Journal of Personality and Social Psychology* 35, no. 9 (1977): 656–666.

28. Interview with P. Eckman, *The New York Times* (August 5, 2003): D5, D8.

29. S. C. Schneider and J. L. Barsoux, *Managing Across Cultures* (Hertfordshire, England: Simon & Schuster International Group, 1997).

30. L. H. Chaney and J. S. Martin, *Intercultural Business Communication,* 3rd ed. (Upper Saddle River, NJ: Pearson Education, 2004).

31. E. Goode, "How Culture Molds Habits of Thought," *The New York Times* (August 8, 2000): D1, D4.

32. Schneider and Barsoux, *supra* n. 29.

33. G. M. Wederspahn, *American Sayings: Foreigners' Windows into US Culture.* Available at http://www.bestbooks.biz/global/american_culture.htm.

34. E. T. Hall, *Beyond Culture* (Garden City, NY: Anchor Books, 1976).

35. Goode, *supra* n. 31.

36. T. Goodman, "Do Men Really Listen with Just Half a Brain? Research Sheds Some Light." Available at http://www.cnn.com/2000/HEALTH/11/28/brain.listening/index.html.

37. D. Tannen, *Talking 9 to 5* (New York: Avon Books, 1995), 43.

38. Ibid., p. 44.

39. Tannen, *supra* n. 37.
40. *The Apprentice,* April 1, 2004. Recap available at http://www.nbc.com/nbc/The_Apprentice/ weekly_recap/week12a.shtml.
41. Tannen, *supra* n. 37.
42. M. Heffernan, "The Female CEO," *Fast Company* (August 2003): 58–66.
43. S. Hite, *Women and Love* (New York: Alfred A. Knopf, 1987).
44. Goodman, *supra* n. 36.
45. Barker and Watson, *supra* n. 11.
46. Ibid.
47. Ibid.
48. Ibid.
49. Floyd, *supra* n. 18.
50. R. Nichols and L. Stevens, "Listening to People," *Harvard Business Review* 35, no. 5 (1957): 85–93.
51. D. G. Myers, *Psychology,* 7th ed. (New York: Worth, 2004).
52. Ibid.
53. Ibid.
54. Ibid.
55. Ibid.
56. "George Burns Quotes." Retrieved February 24, 2004, from http://www.brainyquote.com/quotes/ quotes/g/georgeburn150284.html.
57. Myers, *supra* n. 51.
58. C. Rogers and R. Farson, "Active Listening," in R. G. Newman, M. A. Danziger, and M. Cohen (eds.), *Communicating in Business Today* (Boston: D. C. Heath & Company, 1987).

3 SPECIAL LISTENING OPPORTUNITIES

In the past two chapters of this book, we have advocated strategic listening. We have encouraged you to think about what you want to accomplish through a listening opportunity and then to define effective listening accordingly. We have explored general barriers to listening deeply and how to overcome them. The suggestions offered thus far are useful for dealing with barriers in any listening situation, but to achieve specific listening goals, applying techniques targeting that particular listening goal can be helpful. In this chapter, we discuss special listening opportunities in which you can employ specific strategies in addition to the general tactics discussed in Chapter 2.

LISTENING TO LEARN

Listening to learn is perhaps our first experience with purposeful listening. Although this seems to come naturally (children listen in order to learn to speak), it can be far from easy. A classroom example illustrates some of the challenges for listening with the goal of learning. For a classroom demonstration, a student volunteer is supplied with bread, a jar of peanut butter, a jar of jelly, and a butter knife. Another student volunteer is asked to tell the first student how to make a peanut butter sandwich. It sounds simple enough, but imposing a few rules makes it considerably more difficult. The student making the sandwich is not allowed to ask any questions and is not permitted to do anything unless specifically told to do so. The student giving the instructions isn't allowed to see the student who is making the sandwich. This demonstrates several important points about listening to learn:

- **Assumptions.** It is a rare situation in which a speaker tells us *everything* we need to know. We will—and are expected to—fill in gaps in the information that speakers provide. Speakers will make assumptions about what we already know and how we will fill in what is left out, and as listeners, we make assumptions about how to fill an information gap. In the PB&J exercise, students giving the instructions make assumptions about what the sandwich maker knows to do—such as unscrewing the lid on the peanut butter jar before trying to put the knife in. The sandwich maker usually *would* make assumptions about how to fill in what's not explicitly stated. However, when prevented from doing anything unless instructed, even something as simple as making a sandwich quickly becomes nearly impossible. This illustrates how much we rely on our own ability to fill in information gaps, even when we are trying not to.

- **Feedback.** When we fill in the gaps in incoming information, we might fill them in accordance with the meaning the speaker intended—or we might not. Feedback in the form of questions or perception-checking statements can ensure that we are interpreting information accurately and that our assumptions are correct. Our questions also inform the speaker of what we don't understand, which can help the speaker realize what additional information should be provided. In one demonstration of the sandwich exercise, a student ended up holding two slices of bread, an open jar of peanut butter, the lid from the open jar of peanut butter, and a butter knife in her hands, and was then told to pick up the jar of jelly. Being able to ask the simple question, "Should I set down the jar of peanut butter first?" would have made her work much easier.

- **Nonverbal cues.** We have already discussed the importance of nonverbal cues. When they are absent, we must be alert to the enhanced possibility of misunderstanding. In the sandwich example, if the student giving the instructions were able to observe the student making the sandwich, the process would be greatly simplified.

Over the course of our lifetime, listening is our primary mode of learning. Studies indicate that high school and college students spend from 50 percent to 90 percent of their communication time listening. Not surprisingly, studies also show that students who have effective listening skills are more successful in their academic work than are those who are not good listeners.[1]

What special tactics can you use when your goal is listening to learn? Effective listening to learn requires two things:

- **You must have motivation to stay attentive.** Listening to learn often involves formal listening situations, such as lectures and presentations, where you must listen for long periods of time while someone else speaks. These situations are inherently less interactive, inviting people to lose their concentration. Any time you have to focus your attention on listening for a significant period, you will have many opportunities for your thoughts to wander. Having a clear idea of why you need the information you're listening to can help motivate you to stay focused. Using the lag time between listening and thinking to identify the speaker's purpose, mentally paraphrasing, relating the new information to what you already know, and mentally reviewing and summarizing the material can help you maintain your focus, comprehend the presentation better, and remember more of what is said.[2]

- **You must have ability.** There is no more important time to have a mental framework for organizing new information than when you are listening to learn. Your ability to comprehend and remember what you're listening to depends on your ability to make sense of it initially. Even simple information can seem confusing if you don't have some background information to help you organize it. Read the following passage, or better yet, have someone else read it to you. See how many of the ideas in the paragraph you can recall.

  The procedure is actually quite simple. First you arrange things into groups. Of course, one pile may be sufficient depending on how much there is to do. If you have to go somewhere else due to lack of facilities, that is the next step; otherwise you are pretty well set. It is important not to overdo things. That is, it is better to do too few things at once than too many. In the short run, this may not seem important, but complications can arise. A mistake can prove expensive, as well. At first, the whole procedure will seem complicated. Soon, however, it will become just another facet of life. It is difficult to foresee any end to the necessity for this task in the immediate future, but one can never tell. After the procedure is completed, one arranges the materials into different groups again. Then they can be put into their appropriate places. Eventually they will all be used once more, and the whole cycle will have to be repeated. However, that is part of life.[3]

You will probably find it difficult to recall many ideas from the passage or even comprehend what the passage is about. However, if you had been told that the passage was about washing clothes before reading it, you would probably have been able to remember much more. A study using this paragraph showed that people who were given the title of the passage, "Washing Clothes," before being exposed to the passage were able to remember significantly more of the 18 ideas contained in the paragraph than those who were not given the title. This study illustrates the importance of having a cognitive, or mental, framework in place for understanding and remembering what you listen to. If you know that you will be listening to unfamiliar information, get a little background knowledge before the listening event. If that's not possible, you may have to ask the speaker to provide some background information. Without it, your ability to listen effectively will be compromised.

In addition to motivation and ability, developing certain skills, such as being able to recognize the main points of a speaker's message, taking good notes, and asking the right questions, will be beneficial for listening to learn. Attending to nonverbal cues can help you pick out a speaker's main points. In most listening to learn situations, the content of the message or what the person is actually saying is the most important part of the message, which distinguishes this type of listening from listening situations where empathy with the speaker is desired. Typically, the message won't have much emotional content, and relating to the speaker's feelings is unnecessary. Therefore, paying attention to nonverbal cues will be less about understanding emotions and empathizing with the speaker and more about noticing the emphasis of important points and indications of transitions from one point to another.

Paying too much attention to nonverbal cues in a listening-to-learn situation can actually be a distraction. For example, if you're listening to a speaker who fidgets nervously or speaks in a monotone voice, you can become distracted by evaluating the speaker's delivery rather than focusing on the content of the message. That doesn't mean you should ignore all the nonverbal elements, though. They can help you discern implicit aspects of the message and identify the speaker's purpose, which is sometimes not clearly stated.

Verbal cues also help the listener identify the speaker's main points and the relationships between subpoints. This is particularly helpful in a formal listening situation, where asking questions is often not possible, making it even

Listen to This ▼

"A good listener is not only popular everywhere, but after a while he knows something."[4]
—Wilson Mizner ▲

more critical that the listener attend to the speaker's nonverbal and verbal cues. In their book entitled *Listening,* Wolvin and Coakley identify phrases that are often used by speakers to signify their main idea and words that are commonly used to introduce details, signify transitions, and indicate relationships among points. Some examples are given in the following table.[5]

Phrases Used to Indicate a Main Idea	Words Used to Indicate Relationships Among Points	Words Used to Introduce Details
Tonight I want to talk to you about . . . To summarize . . . Simply stated . . . What's important here . . .	Therefore Because Since First, second Next Finally	For instance To explain The fact is Namely To illustrate To describe

TAKING NOTES

During lectures or meetings, many people take notes. Taking notes prompts us to summarize the information we're hearing, and later, our notes serve as a record of that information. Note taking can improve our ability to concentrate. Many students report that taking notes helps them stay focused on a lecture. Note taking also helps us recognize patterns, transitions, main ideas, and the general organization of a message as we try to organize our notes. It helps us put messages in long-term memory by forcing us to work with the information and think about it. Of course, the most effective way for note taking to improve our memory is for us to refer to our notes later.

There are numerous note-taking methods. One mistake that note takers sometimes make is trying to write down everything they hear. But it's really not possible to write down things as quickly as people can speak (unless you're skilled at the lost art of shorthand). Trying to do so merely causes note takers to become frustrated and miss much of what is said. Rather than trying to write down everything, a method of note taking should be employed that can help you accomplish your listening goals. The best method depends on the type of information you're listening to, how the speaker has organized it, what you want to get from it, and your own personal preferences. Whatever method you use, highlighting important information or main points so that everything on the page doesn't look the same will help you get the most out of your notes. You can highlight text by using underlining or circling, using all capital letters, or using any way that works for you.

Some popular methods for note taking include:[6]

- **Outlining.** Outlining is a common form of note taking, and outlines, because of how they are organized, are easy to use. They help us identify relationships between main points and supporting material. However, it can be difficult to create an outline for material that isn't presented with some clear form of organization (and less than half of all speeches are). Furthermore, listeners can sometimes become preoccupied with formatting the outline and miss some of what is said.
- **Enumeration.** One way to organize your notes is to number the points. This is a practical approach of jotting down the main ideas and numbering them (an especially sensible method when the speaker is presenting numbered points).

- ■ **Mapping method.** The mapping or clustering method is a more visual technique for taking notes and can be particularly useful when messages are disorganized. Mapping involves writing main ideas on the paper as they are presented and circling them. Supporting details are written on lines that connect to the circles or in smaller circles clustered around the circled main idea.

SKILLED QUESTIONING

When it's possible, such as in a meeting or a small class, an important part of listening to learn is asking good questions. A clear benefit to asking questions is that it allows for the listener to get needed information. Another clear benefit is that questions improve the understanding achieved between speaker and listener. As noted in Chapter 2, asking questions gives listeners a chance to clarify their understanding. It communicates interest to the speaker and allows the speaker to determine whether the listener really is understanding what has been said.

Asking questions, however, actually yields a great deal more than these fairly obvious benefits. Questions, asked the right way, can get people to open up, giving them a chance to grow their relationships and build trust. Managers can learn what motivates their employees, stimulate employee thinking, and encourage employee participation in the organization through asking questions. In conflicts, asking questions is an important part of the resolution process. Through questions we can come to understand another party's interests and goals. We can gain insight into the reasons for a person's disagreement with our position. Understanding what prevents someone from agreeing with us or discovering the basis for a person's objections can help us produce solutions that overcome them.

People ask questions for different purposes, and different types of questions accomplish different things. Questions fall into one of two basic categories: open-ended or close-ended. Open-ended questions require more than a few simple words to answer. They are asked in order to draw out more information from the speaker. They often begin with words such as "How" or "What." Close-ended questions, on the other hand, can typically be answered with a "yes" or "no" or other response of a few words. Close-ended questions are often used for fact finding.

Listen to This ▼

"Who questions much, shall learn much, and retain much." [7]
—Francis Bacon ▲

Examples of Open-Ended Questions
What's your reaction to the plan?
How do you feel about that idea?
What do you think we should do?

Examples of Close-Ended Questions
Did you order the new machine?
Did you work over the weekend?
How many people attended the meeting?

In addition to determining the type of question you should ask, the following considerations can contribute to your successful use of questions:[8]

- **Setting the stage.** Be sure the person has time to talk. If a person doesn't really have the time to talk, then it's a bad time to ask open-ended questions. Under time constraints, people will typically make their responses as brief as possible, even if the questions are open ended. In some cases, you may want to ask permission to ask questions. This isn't always necessary, but it can help the speaker trust your motives for asking and thus open up more.

- **Have a questioning plan.** A questioning plan is a general idea of the questions you will ask. That doesn't mean that you must pin down the exact wording of your questions in advance. You won't always want to pull out a piece of paper with questions on it, as you might in an interview, but having a general idea of the type of question you will ask can help ensure that you obtain the information you're after. Even though you want to have a questioning plan before you begin, your questions should build on previous responses. When you've listened to an answer, your next question should reflect that in some way. Generally, questions should move from broad to narrow. Answering broad questions first will get the speaker to open up and be more willing to answer narrower questions.

Although asking questions can be quite useful, it is possible to ask questions in a way that does more harm than good. Here are some suggestions for things to avoid when asking questions:

- **Avoid making statements disguised as questions.** When someone asks questions that begin with phrases such as "Don't you think that . . ." or "Shouldn't you . . ." or "Wouldn't it be better if . . ." the answer that the person hopes to get is built into the question. These are really statements disguised as questions. If you want to hear what the other person thinks, rather than asking something like, "Don't you think we should use our current vendor?" ask, "Do you think we should use our current vendor?"

- **Avoid asking questions that begin with "why."** By their very nature, questions that begin with "why" put the respondent on the defensive. Questions such as "Why did you do that?" ask the respondent to defend an action. We often ask "why" questions without intentionally trying to put a person on the defensive; however, defensiveness is a natural reaction to a "why" question. Sometimes we really do want to understand why a person did a certain thing or made a certain choice, so what do we do then? "Why" questions can be reworded in such a way that "why" information is shared without the defensiveness. For example, instead of asking, "Why did you do that?" you could ask, "What led you to take that route?" This alters the focus of the question from the speaker's behavior and the defense of it to the factors that contributed to it.

- **Avoid debating the person's answer to your questions, especially if the person is giving a viewpoint you've asked to hear.** Leading questions and statements disguised as questions often appear in the conversation when we attempt to argue with the opinion we've just asked to hear. We may ask, "Do you think we should use our old vendor?" and then respond to an answer of "Yes" with a question such as, "Don't you think we could get a better deal from a new one?" The speaker might be wondering at this point, "If you didn't want to know my thoughts, why did you ask to hear them?"

- **Avoid asking too many questions about irrelevant details.** Asking questions about irrelevant details can make speakers feel like you're missing the real point of what they're saying.

Listening to learn can be challenging because the information you're listening to may lack emotional content to engage or entertain you. In addition, listening to learn often occurs in formal

> **Thought Box**
>
> 1. What type of information do you find easy to organize and listen to? What strategies can you use to improve your ability to organize and comprehend information that is difficult, technical, or novel?
>
> 2. What method of note taking do you usually use? Do you typically review your notes regularly when learning something new, or are you more likely to review your notes only when you're going to be tested on the information? How effective are your note-taking and review processes? What can you do to improve their effectiveness?
>
> 3. As an employee, have you been listened to empathically? What effect did it have on you?

listening situations, where the information is likely to be presented by a speaker who may not be particularly gifted and with whom you have no personal connection. Being aware of your listening goal, gaining any necessary background knowledge, taking notes, and asking good questions can help you improve in this important skill.

LISTENING TO PERSUASIVE MESSAGES

We are bombarded regularly with messages meant to influence our beliefs, attitudes, or behaviors. When we are making decisions, it is important for us to be critical consumers of persuasive information. But often we fail to do evaluative listening and are influenced by poor arguments or factors unrelated to actual evidence. It has long been known that we are persuaded by more than just arguments and evidence. Aristotle called the elements of persuasion ethos, pathos, and logos, with the most persuasive messages including components of all three.

- **Ethos** refers to the charisma or personal credibility of the speaker.
- **Pathos** refers to the values, psychological needs, and emotions of the person being persuaded.
- **Logos** refers to the logical arguments presented to persuade.

Social influence is the more general term that refers to the influence of one person or group of persons on the beliefs, attitudes, or behaviors on another. The spectrum of social influence includes conformity, compliance, obedience, and persuasion. Although some researchers include all forms of social influence as persuasion, many see important distinctions among them. These researchers distinguish persuasion from other forms of social influence in part by considering whether or not the change in the receiver of a persuasive message is internalized. In other words, they ask the question, "Has the receiver of the message really changed his position, or is he just outwardly acting as if he has?" In a case of true persuasion, the listener would have actually changed his mind.

We are all influenced by others in ways that do not result in internalized change:

- **Compliance.** Compliance means we agree to a direct request, but that doesn't necessarily mean we've internalized a change. We may agree to go to a coworker's favorite spot for lunch, even though we don't care for the place, simply because the coworker begs us to go there. Agreeing to go doesn't mean we've changed our attitude about the restaurant; it simply means we are complying with our coworker's request.
- **Obedience.** Similarly, we may do something our boss has told us to do—even if we think it's a really bad idea. Doing what we're told doesn't mean that we have suddenly decided the boss's idea is a good one—it simply means that we perceive the boss to have power over us regarding work matters. This sort of obedience, again, falls short of true persuasion.
- **Conformity.** Conformity occurs when we change in accordance to a norm for our social group. Sometimes we conform in ways we would really rather not, but we do so anyway to maintain our position in the group.

Persuasion, on the other hand, refers to an actual, internalized change. We've made a change in our beliefs, attitudes, or behavior, not to please someone else or because we feel we have to, but because we really believe in the change. We may think that we would experience true persuasion only when we have listened carefully to a message and found it to be convincing. Surprisingly, however, we can experience this type of change and be truly persuaded by messages without really listening to them at all.

When we listen to persuasive messages, we can proceed along one of two mental pathways for processing the information. Along one pathway, we listen deeply to the persuasive message, carefully evaluating the evidence and weighing the strength of the arguments presented. With this deep-level processing, sometimes called *central route processing,* we invest our energy into thinking critically about the message and comparing it with what we already know or believe. If, after all this mental work, we find the argument credible, we will be genuinely persuaded. We will internalize our new position and will be more likely to hold that position over time and in the face of future arguments against it.[9]

Alternatively, we can make a decision about a persuasive message while paying very little attention to the arguments. Instead we can look to other aspects of the communication system to help us make up our minds. This pathway to processing, sometimes called *peripheral route processing,* allows us to look for simple cues to help us make up our minds about a message, without having to invest energy into thinking deeply about the message content. For example, a person might look at the source of a message, find

> **Listen to This** ▼
>
> *"The moment we want to believe something, we suddenly see all the arguments for it, and become blind to the arguments against it."* [11]
>
> —George Bernard Shaw ▲

the source credible, and then follow the recommendation of the source without paying attention to the arguments offered in support of the recommendations. In that case, credibility would be a peripheral cue.[10]

Various aspects of the elements in the communication system can serve as peripheral cues for listeners:[12]

- **Sender.** A number of characteristics of the sender can serve as a peripheral cue. In general, these characteristics could be lumped together and called credibility. But a sender need not possess all the components of credibility to be persuasive. Any one of them can serve as a peripheral cue. *Expertise* can be a cue. ("If the expert says it is so, it must be so.") Doctors are a good example of experts who are listened to uncritically. But doctors make mistakes and sometimes make recommendations that are not based on sound science. Infomercials selling vitamins that promise to reverse the aging process or heal a variety of ills often feature a medical doctor's endorsement in lieu of empirical evidence. Listeners are often persuaded by the *M.D.* behind the endorser's name and don't focus on the quality of the evidence and arguments presented in the message. *Likability* can be persuasive. ("If I like this person and he thinks this is a good idea, it probably is.") Advertisers know that appealing personalities and attractive faces can persuade people to buy products, even without an accompanying explanation of the products' features and benefits. *Similarity* can also be a cue. ("This person is so much like me, if she likes this, I will as well.") The "plain folks" appeal, which emphasizes the similarities between the speaker and the listener, is used to help listeners feel a connection with the speaker. Political campaigns are often rife with, "I'm just like you" messages.
- **Message.** Aspects of the message, outside its actual content, can serve as a peripheral cue. For example, when coming from a credible source, complex arguments that use jargon or words that are difficult to understand can be a cue. When we're not listening carefully to a source we tend to trust, the more complicated the message, the more convincing it can be. Even the number of arguments, without respect to their content, can be a cue. As when grading term papers by their weight, we sometimes disregard the quality of arguments in favor of noting only the quantity of them.
- **Context.** Aspects of the environment can serve as social cues. For example, if you are listening to a presentation and people around you are smiling and nodding their heads in agreement with the speaker, you may use their signs of agreement as social proof that you should accept the speaker's message as well.

When persuaded by a peripheral cue, the persuasion is genuine in that it represents an internalized change in the listener. However, persuasion by peripheral-route processing is generally less enduring than persuasion through central-route processing. Because this type of persuasion is not based on sound evidence and reasoning, it usually doesn't endure the tests of time or well-constructed counterarguments.

Using peripheral cues to make a decision, instead of listening critically, offers the advantage of saving you some mental energy, but it harbors the risk of you making a poor decision. Experts can be wrong, and likable people don't always have your best interests at heart. More arguments don't necessarily make a case stronger, and people who use words you don't understand may not know what they're talking about. When a decision is important, you need to invest the energy to listen critically.

So when do we, as listeners, take the central route to persuasion, and when do we take the peripheral route? In general, people are motivated to hold correct beliefs or attitudes, but people also tend to be what is often called "cognitive misers." This means that people would generally prefer to expend as little mental energy as necessary to make good decisions about correct beliefs or attitudes. For most people, the possibility of taking a shortcut to making a decision and still being reasonably sure of making a correct one is pretty appealing. Of course, this is a generality and doesn't hold true for everyone. Some people enjoy engaging in demanding mental work and, therefore, wouldn't choose a shortcut even if one were available.[13]

In general, listeners need two things in order to listen critically and process information deeply: motivation and ability (see Figure 3.1). Motivation can be affected by a number of factors. If a topic is important and personally consequential, people are more likely to be motivated to process it deeply. You may not pay much attention to the arguments for redistricting a school system unless your children are in school there. You may not process arguments for increasing the minimum wage unless you are a small business owner who has a large number of 16- and 17-year-olds working for you. Recognizing that a message involves personal consequences can be motivating.

Ability can also be affected by a number of factors, including many of those mentioned previously as processing barriers. A listener may lack the background knowledge to process a message effectively, major levels of distraction in the environment could make it difficult to hear or

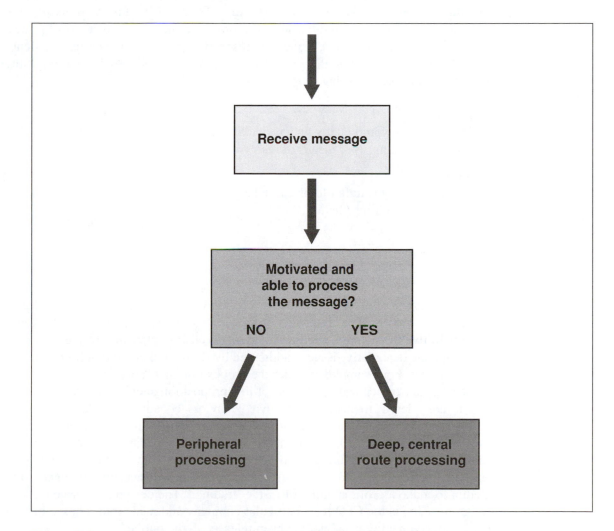

Figure 3.1   To listen critically we need motivation and ability

to concentrate, or language differences could create a communication barrier.[14] We can improve our ability to listen critically to persuasive arguments by becoming familiar with the structure of arguments and being able to recognize various parts of an argument. As listeners, we often don't have the luxury of reviewing arguments repeatedly (as we might if we were *reading* a persuasive message); therefore, our ability to quickly recognize and deconstruct an argument is imperative.

The parts of an argument consist of an assertion or a series of assertions, supported by evidence and woven together by reasoning. For example, "I deserve this promotion" is an assertion. "I deserve this promotion because I have the best sales record" is an assertion supported by evidence.

Assertions or propositions can be of fact, value, or policy. Propositions of fact argue that something is or isn't, was or wasn't, or will or will not be. Propositions of value argue that something is good or bad, right or wrong, moral or immoral. Propositions of policy argue that a change should or shouldn't be made or that something should or shouldn't be done.

A Google search using the search terms "NAFTA" and "Social Security" produced Web sites containing the following propositions:

Fact
Privatization would fatally undermine Social Security.
NAFTA has improved means of resolving trade disputes.

Value
Social Security is unfair to black males.
NAFTA is good for Mexico.

Policy
We need to privatize Social Security.
NAFTA's unfair trade policies should be changed.

For each type of proposition, standard issues, or *stock issues,* should be addressed before the argument is accepted. For arguments of fact and value, stock issues are definitive and designative. Definitive issues are addressed by giving a clear explanation of the terms in the proposition, while the designative issue is addressed by showing that the requirements in the definition have been met. For example, consider the proposition that "John is guilty of insider trading." A message meant to persuade us to accept this proposition should include a clear explanation of who is considered an insider and what behaviors constitute insider trading (the definitive issues). The argument should also present evidence that John engaged in the required behavior (the designative issue). So, the definitive issues might be addressed by stating, "The SEC considers anyone privy to information not yet made public, who is expected to maintain the confidentiality of the information, to be an insider. A person who acts on privileged information in an attempt to make a profit is guilty of insider trading." The designative issue might be addressed by stating, "Joe is the CFO for a particular company and made trades based on a positive earnings announcement that had not yet been released to the public."[16]

For propositions of policy, a speaker should provide the listener with evidence that a problem exists, a statement of the solution, proof that the solution is practical and would actually solve the problem, and a description of the advantages and disadvantages of the solution. Consider, for example, the following claim:[17]

We should implement an onsite day-care program because, according to human resources, 40 percent of our absenteeism is caused by child-care issues.

Listening to this argument, we may find it initially persuasive. If we're listening critically, we will recognize the assertion or proposition as, "We should implement an onsite day care program" and the evidence as, "Child-care issues account for 40 percent of absenteeism." Although this gives us evidence of a problem, it falls short of addressing all the stock issues. We don't know, for example, whether an onsite day-care facility is really a practical option. Furthermore, we can't be certain that the "child-care issues" reported as a reason for absenteeism will be solved by having an onsite day-care center. For example, if "child-care issues" refer primarily to an ill child, onsite day care may not help much. It may not help at all if "child-care issues" really means, "I'd rather go to the beach than go to work today."

Arguments often make sense only to the extent to which certain assumptions are held by both the speaker and the listener. These (often implicit) parts of an argument are called warrants, and they serve to connect the evidence to the claim. Warrants are the general beliefs or assumptions we must hold in order for the evidence to support the claim in a way that makes sense. Speakers often take for granted that their listeners share these assumptions or cultural beliefs and may therefore make them an implicit or unspoken part of their argument. For example, for the claim, "We should implement an onsite day-care program because, according to human resources, 40 percent of our absenteeism is caused by child-care issues," the unspoken warrant is, "These issues would be solved by an onsite day-care program."

Consider the claim, "Company X will make a fortune from this product because it actually helps people lose weight no matter how much they eat." If we are listening to this claim and are at all familiar with American culture, then we don't need the person making the claim to explain to us that being thin is highly valued in the United States—and so is eating—and that many Americans struggle with their weight. Yet it is only with this knowledge that we can see how a product that helps people lose weight could mean huge profits for a company.[18]

The warrant makes the evidence relevant to the assertion, and thus, we must accept the warrant to accept the argument. Consider the claim "Sean shouldn't get the promotion because he's too young." Upon hearing this claim, we may wonder about the relevance of the evidence because the warrant is a bit unclear. The warrant for this speaker might be that young people can't handle responsibility. Or it might be that clients won't be willing to accept someone so young in such a position. To evaluate the relevance of the evidence, we may need to ask some questions about the warrant to determine whether we agree with it (e.g., what bothers you about his age?). If we reject the warrant (as we might with the belief that young people can't handle responsibility), the speaker will need to have additional evidence to persuade us.

Listening critically to evidence entails more than evaluating relevance. As critical listeners, we also want to carefully consider the quality of any relevant evidence offered by a speaker. A reasonable place to start is by determining whether the evidence presented is fact, inference, or opinion. A fact is a conclusive piece of evidence. It can be proven, typically, because it is publicly observable. An inference is a judgment based on facts, but it is not in itself a fact. If you look outside your window and see that it's raining and say, "It's raining," that is a statement of fact. When the meteorologist on your local news program says that it will rain in the morning, that is an inference. He or she bases this inference on facts from available equipment and the interpretation of those facts using his or her expertise. Inferences are not always correct. It may or may not rain in the morning. So the degree to which we count on an inference being right will depend on how confident we are in someone's ability to interpret facts.

Opinions are views, judgments, or peripheral beliefs. Opinions can be quite strong but are not necessarily based on anything more than the judgment of the person forming the opinion. The opinions of formally trained experts or people highly experienced in an area can be used as evidence; however, they are not the best form of evidence. As listeners, it is important to note the distinction between the quality of evidence represented by facts, inferences, and opinions. Equally important is realizing the lack of distinction in the way that speakers refer to each of these. It is not uncommon for people to talk about their opinions and inferences as if they were, indeed, facts. For example, "The fact of the matter is that Sean is simply too young to get that promotion." Or, "There is no doubt this product will be a big seller."

Listen to This ▼

"There are as many opinions as there are experts." [19]
—Franklin D. Roosevelt ▲

You might also evaluate evidence based on whether it is one of the following:[20]

- **Accurate.** Evidence that is inaccurate is not particularly valuable. When you are listening to evidence, you must evaluate its accuracy to the extent that you are able.
  > *I deserve this promotion because I've cut costs in our department by 10 percent every year for the past three years.*
  If you know the person has reduced departmental spending by 10 percent but that it was a result of a restructuring that centralized many administrative duties and reduced costs for all departments by about that amount, then this evidence wouldn't give an accurate picture of the speaker's achievement.
- **Precise.** Good evidence is precise. It is unambiguous and doesn't leave the listener with unanswered questions.
  > *I deserve this promotion because I've reduced costs in this department every year for five years.*
  This argument sounds pretty impressive, but it lacks precision. We may wonder how much costs have been reduced and during which years.
- **Sufficient.** Evidence must provide enough reason to lead to the conclusion it supports.
  > *I deserve this promotion because I've been in the department longer than anyone else.*
  This argument makes sense, but only if you accept the idea that seniority is a good enough reason for promotion.
- **Representative.** A single vivid example can be very persuasive. As listeners, we can get swept up by the emotion of an engaging story. But an engaging anecdote may not reflect the *typical* story. Anecdotal evidence lacks representativeness.
  Statistics from biased samples are also not representative. As listeners, we frequently pay little attention to information about how a statistic was derived. We've all seen the familiar television commercials that state, "Four out of five dentists recommend Trident for their patients who chew gum." Listeners wondering about the representativeness of

this evidence might ask the questions "Were only five dentists surveyed?" and "How were the dentists selected?" Recently, Trident has run a humorous series of ads about the five dentists, answering another question one might ask, "What about the fifth dentist?" In the ads, something outrageous happens to the fifth dentist just as the recommendations are about to be made. In a 15-second spot titled "The Fifth Dentist" that ran during Super Bowl XXXVII, a squirrel runs up the pants leg of the fifth dentist just as he is about to give his recommendation.

> *I deserve this promotion because I did such a great job with the Landers campaign.*

If we know the speaker did well on the Landers campaign, we may find this evidence compelling. However, before we are persuaded by it, we should evaluate its representativeness. Perhaps the speaker did well with the one account, but does that reflect the general quality of his or her work?

- **Understandable.** If we are really listening, we will want to be able to understand evidence clearly and relate it to the argument as evidence. In some cases, speakers purposely create confusing messages in their attempt to persuade others.

Many arguments will include qualifiers that specify conditions when the evidence supports the claim or a degree of uncertainty about the claim. Qualifiers help listeners realize the limits of an argument. But critical listeners can get valuable insight by attending to a *lack* of qualifiers.

Words such as *always* or *never* are red flags for listeners. It's rare for extremes such as *always* or *never* to be accurate.

Listen to This▼

"I feel less prone to make definitive statements about what is right or wrong. I am more likely to acknowledge the importance of stance, power, influence, trendiness." [21]
—Howard Gardner ▲

Using extreme words such as *always* and *never* is only one of many ways to bias an argument. Persuasive messages built on biased arguments are considered to be propaganda. Propaganda is persuasion, but with biased arguments. Critical listeners should be aware of commonly used propaganda techniques so that they can recognize them when they hear them. A number of propaganda techniques are used to get listeners to buy into an argument without really evaluating its quality. Some of the more common techniques are described next.[22]

- **Word games.** We have noted the power of the word to shape perceptions. Propagandists recognize the power of words, and many are experts at carefully choosing words to create in their listeners the kind of response they want.
  - **Name calling.** Applying labels to individuals or groups can shape an unsuspecting listener's attitudes. If someone is called a radical, a nerd, a yuppie, a feminazi, or a tree hugger, we begin to create an image of what that person is like based on the label applied to them.
  - **Glittering generalities.** Words can represent deeply held virtues (e.g., freedom, justice). When these words are used, they can create positive reactions in the minds of listeners without the presence of real evidence. Before the scandal, Kenneth Lay, Enron's chairman and CEO, stated, "Our world-class employees and their commitment to innovative ideas continue to drive our success in today's fast-paced business environment."[23]

- **Euphemisms.** Euphemisms make something unpleasant sound a bit more acceptable by using different words. For example, companies may "downsize" or "rightsize," female singers may experience a "wardrobe malfunction," and cows may be "depopulated" when there is a risk of disease.

- **False connections**
  - **Transfer.** This involves attempting to get the listener to associate something that is already valued with something that the propagandist wants the listener to accept. For example, in Western society, science is highly valued. Over-the-counter diet pills, supplements that increase brain power, and creams that make wrinkles disappear are often promoted with ads that include scientific language, even though the ads don't refer to any genuine scientific evidence.
  - **Testimonials.** There is nothing wrong with a qualified expert giving his or her testimonial as evidence. Who is considered a qualified expert depends on the person and the issue. Testimonials become propaganda when the person offering testimony really has no special experience or training related to the issue. Celebrities who publicly endorse political candidates provide a good example of this type of propaganda. For the most part, there is no reason to believe that a television or film star is wiser than other people in political matters.

- **Special Appeals**
  - **Bandwagon.** The "everyone is doing it, so you should, too" appeal is often successful because we all have an underlying need to be socially accepted. Often this appeal is presented with an urgency that feels like the train is about to leave the station and you're going to be the only one left standing on the platform. Often the social acceptance isn't what it's presented to be. And even if it is, our parents had a good point when they asked us, "If Joe jumped off a bridge, would you do it, too?"
  - **Fear.** Such appeals are meant to arouse fear in the listeners. The speaker then offers them a way of dealing with the threat. Like many propaganda techniques, fear appeals are not inherently bad. Many social service campaigns include fear appeals that are designed to encourage people to fear things that they should rightly be afraid of, such as AIDS or the health consequences of smoking. Fear appeals are propagandist when they exaggerate a threat to exploit the fear of the listener or misrepresent the effectiveness of their recommendation for dealing with the threat.

DETECTING DECEPTION

For most of us, listening to someone we don't really trust and sorting out what we believe is the truth from what we think might be a lie is a difficult task. Most of us believe we're pretty good at determining whether someone is telling us a lie, but research suggests we're not nearly as good as we think we are. One reason is that we look for the wrong cues to deception. When asked how we can tell whether someone is lying, a common answer is "eye contact." If someone can't "look us in the eye," we suspect that he or she might be lying. But research shows that this is not the best cue. In fact, people may actually engage in more eye contact when they lie.[24] Perhaps it's not surprising, then, that most people attempting to detect a lie are no more accurate than they would be if they simply tossed a coin.

Listen to This ▼

"Marge, it takes two to lie. One to lie and one to listen." [25]
—Homer Simpson ▲

If we were better at telling when a person is lying, we might be surprised at how often it occurs. Studies indicate that on average, people lie nearly every day. People lie for a variety reasons that fall into three main categories:[26]

- **Self-interest lies.** People may lie to protect themselves from harm, to make themselves appear "better" than they really are, to gain some benefit for themselves, to avoid conflict, or to avoid an invasion of privacy.
- **Other-interest lies.** People may lie to protect others from harm or to compliment others.
- **Harmful lies.** People may lie to harm others.

Lies typically take the form of omission of information, distortion of information, giving false information, or some combination of any or all these. For example, imagine in a casual conversation around the water cooler that the head of your department asks you how the project your team is working on is progressing. The team has had some very productive meetings, but currently, the team is facing some conflicts, and progress has slowed to a near stop. You're confident, however, that your team will be able to work through the conflicts shortly and move ahead. In addition, you have great faith in the project manager, who happens to be a very good friend. So how do you respond the department head's question?[27]

- **An open and honest answer** might be, "Well, we're experiencing some conflict right now that has slowed things down, but I'm confident we'll be back on track shortly."
- **A lie of omission** might be, "We've had some really great meetings, really productive."
- **A lie of distortion** might be, "The different perspectives are really contributing something to this group. I think we're going to produce a spectacular outcome."
- **A lie of falsification** might be, "Everything is going great. We're cruising along."

Michael Wheeler, professor of management at Harvard University, suggests that we can improve our ability to detect deception by listening with all our senses to catch microexpressions where lying leaks out and by listening all the time instead of focusing on what we're going to say.[28] Cues to deception are both verbal and nonverbal. Unfortunately, for those attempting to detect deception, no one cue or set of cues is a reliable indicator for all people. As it turns out, the only consistent finding across different types of studies is that nonverbal cues are usually better indicators of deception than verbal cues. In general, liars show the following differences from those telling the truth:[29]

Verbal
Make more speech errors
Deliver shorter messages
Include less irrelevant information in their message
Include more negative expressions in their message
Use more generalized terms
Have more discrepancies in their message

> **Thought Box**
>
> 1. What are the most powerful peripheral cues for you?
>
> 2. What topics motivate you to listen critically? What can you do to motivate yourself to listen critically to topics that don't naturally motivate you?
>
> 3. How do you detect deception in a casual business acquaintance? What makes a person seem trustworthy in an initial meeting? What makes you suspicious that a person can't be trusted?

Nonverbal
Blink more
Fidget more
Shrug more
Have more hesitations in their speech
Use a more anxious pitch

Listening critically to persuasive messages can be a difficult but worthwhile task. Messages designed to influence us will not always be delivered by knowledgeable speakers who have our best interest at heart. When the decision matters, we must listen critically to persuasive messages and evaluate the evidence presented.

LISTENING TO CONFLICT

Many people have negative attitudes toward conflict. Listening to the way people talk about conflict and the metaphors they use bears that out. Phrases such as "at each other's throats," "butting heads," "blowing up," or "losing it" make conflict sound extremely unpleasant and possibly even frightening and beyond our control.

Wise managers know, however, that conflict doesn't have to be a bad thing. The belief that conflict is always negative and should be avoided is a myth. The belief that conflict *can* be avoided is another myth. Conflict is inevitable, even in the best of relationships. And although destructive conflicts certainly can be negative experiences, constructive conflicts can produce positive outcomes. Destructive conflicts increase competition between people, don't really solve problems, tend to be very emotional, and weaken relationships. Constructive conflicts, on the other hand, increase cooperation, solve problems, and avoid personal and emotional attacks. In fact, constructive conflicts can actually improve relationships.

Listen to This ▼

"Whenever you're in conflict with someone, there is one factor that can make the difference between damaging your relationship and deepening it. That factor is attitude." [30]
—William James ▲

Through communication, we initiate, maintain, escalate, and work through conflict. Importantly, through communication, conflict becomes destructive or constructive. Effective listening is the single most important communication skill for keeping conflicts constructive and resolving them effectively.

Conflict occurs when people (or parties, to use conflict resolution lingo) perceive themselves to have incompatible goals. When we think of goals that can be the source of conflict, we may initially think of what are known as content goals. Content goals are about resources and how they are distributed or about outcomes of an event. Parties may want the same resource, but there might not be enough of it to go around. For example, two people share an office, and only one can have the desk by the window. Or two managers want to travel to a client's base of operations, but the travel budget allows for only one of them to go. Or the content goal can be about the outcome of an event. Two managers may prefer two different vendors, but only one can be chosen.

Content goals may be the first sort of goal that comes to mind when we think about conflicts at work, but there are others. Other types of goals include process goals, relational goals, and identity goals. *Process goals* are about how things are done and how communication occurs. For example, conflicts over process goals occur when parties don't agree about the type or amount of communication or who should be included in the communication. A person may be upset about being left "out of the loop." Conflicts over *relational goals* occur when parties define their relationship differently. For example, a male and female coworker may have different desires for the nature of their relationship. The male coworker may want to have a personal relationship with the female coworker outside of work, while the female coworker may prefer to keep the relationship strictly professional. *Identity goals* are about how we see ourselves and how we think others view us. Conflicts over identity goals occur when others view us differently from how we view ourselves. If we think we are competent and hardworking, we would like others to view us in this same way. If a coworker views us as incompetent and lazy, we are likely to have a conflict over our identity goal.

As listeners, understanding different goals helps us identify what is really driving a conflict—which is not always easy. Different types of goals can make a conflict more or less easy to work through for several reasons. First, some types of goals naturally have more emotional involvement than others, and intense emotions can complicate efforts to resolve conflict. For example, conflicts over content goals may have only minor levels of emotional involvement if the resource at issue is not terribly important. On the other hand, conflicts about relational or identity goals are likely to involve more emotion.

Second, some goals are more readily identifiable than others. One reason for this is that some goals are more likely to be directly expressed. We typically have little problem expressing our interests when it comes to content goals, but we are sometimes hesitant to "lay it on the line" when our concerns are over relational or identity issues. Without direct expression of these goals, however, listeners must attempt to hear what's *not* being said and ask good questions to get to the heart of the conflict.

Finally, some goals are easier for the parties themselves to understand than other goals are. Not only are we less likely to openly express some of our goals, but some goals are difficult for us to recognize and understand. We have probably all been in conflict situations where even we were surprised by how upset we were getting. At some level, we may wonder, "Where is this coming from?" Or we may simply decide that we care about the issue at hand more than we originally thought. In some cases, the real reason for the depth of our emotion is an unmet goal we may not be completely aware of at the moment. For example, imagine two coworkers, Jane and Kelly, who have different ideas about the best location for an important conference with several clients. Jane argues the advantages of her location feverishly, in part because she genuinely prefers her location, but part of her fervor is a result of her identity goals of being extremely smart and right nearly all the time. In the moment of the argument, she may not be really be thinking about these goals, but she will feel the effects of them in her level of intensity. Even if Jane becomes aware of the fact that these other goals are operating, she isn't likely to say, "You should agree with me because I want you to think I'm smarter than you."

Like Jane's situation, most conflicts, in fact, will involve multiple goals. Goals can appear in any combination and can be of varying importance. Still, despite the presence of multiple issues, when parties raise their concerns, they will frequently speak only about the content or process goals at issue. They will be less likely to bring up their identity and relational concerns, whether they are aware of them or not. This, of course, adds to the already significant challenge of listening effectively during conflict.

COMMON PITFALLS TO AVOID WHEN LISTENING TO CONFLICTS

The challenge of listening effectively during a conflict is intensified even further by the course that conflict conversations often take. The typical conflict begins like this:

1. One party raises an issue with another by pointing out to that party "the error of his or her ways."
2. The errant party then responds defensively and proceeds to counterattack.
3. The parties then argue back and forth, attempting to get each other to admit wrongdoing.
4. Emotions may escalate and tempers may flare, leading to name calling or other destructive behavior.

This "going nowhere" cycle is common, ineffective, and easily turned around by good listening. When listening to conflict, the effective listener must overcome the temptation to blame, argue, and make negative inferences.

THE PROBLEM WITH BLAME

The tendency to fix blame in a conflict comes from our one-sided view of a conflict. When we raise an issue with another person, we are usually certain of two things: We are in the right, and the other person is in the wrong. Fixing blame, then, stems from our desire to help the other person realize his or her "wrongness" and perhaps to offer recommendations for correcting it along the way. This strategy, common as it may be, is usually not effective. Most people aren't eager to shoulder blame, especially if they feel the blame is unjustified. The other party is likely to respond defensively to statements of his or her "wrongness" and will likely try to show how the accuser is really the one at fault.[31]

For all parties in a conflict, the tendency is to focus on speaking rather than listening. When we

Listen to This ▼

"The longer we ruminate about what has made us angry, the more 'good reasons' and self-justifications for being angry we can invent." [32]
—Daniel Goleman ▲

confront people because we think they've done us wrong, we are far more likely to be focused on talking instead of listening. We often think we are clear about who did what and who is to blame. Similarly, when others confront us about what they think we have done wrong and we are feeling defensive, we are far more likely to turn our attention to speaking in our own defense instead of listening.

THE PROBLEM WITH ARGUING

The effort to fix blame can deteriorate into arguing as soon as an issue is raised. Arguing is often no more than an attempt, back and forth between the parties, to affix blame and assign fault. The problem here is that both parties are arguing and no one is listening. Arguing without listening doesn't accomplish anything. People will tend to repeat the same things, over and over again, because they know they aren't being heard.

Another problem with arguing is that people tend to argue their conclusions about what happened and why, without explaining how they arrived at their conclusions (and because the other party isn't really listening, no explanation is requested).[33] People in conflict may draw wildly different conclusions about what happened and who did what. This can lead to confusion and more arguing because the conclusions are viewed as wrong. People have different conclusions for several reasons, including the following:

- **Different information.** We are frequently exposed to different information than the other party in a conflict. For example, you may be in a conflict with someone who works in a different office or a different department, and thus, the two of you have access to varying information. However, even when we are all exposed to the same information, we may individually select different aspects of that to pay attention to. For example, you and a colleague may attend the same meeting, and while you are paying close attention to every word that is said, your colleague may be paying equally close attention to the nonverbal behavior of the senior decision maker. As a result, the two of you walk away from the same meeting with different information about what happened in the meeting.
- **Different interpretation.** Sharing the same information doesn't mean we'll have the same interpretation of it as someone else. As we have already discussed, myriad factors influence our perceptions. If, in the example above, you and your colleague both pay attention to the senior decision maker's nonverbal cues, cultural differences between the two of you may lead you to think the reaction is positive but lead your colleague to view it as negative.
- **Different interests.** Whether we intend for them to or not, our conclusions reflect our self-interests. A professor at Harvard Business School demonstrated this effect when he gave student teams either the role of seller of a business or buyer of a business. After assigning the roles, he asked the teams to estimate the value of the business (*not* the price they would *ask* or be willing to *pay,* but the objective value). He found that for teams selling the business, the estimates were about 30 percent more than the assessed fair market value. For teams buying the business, on the other hand, the value of the business was estimated at 30 percent less than its assessed value.[34]

When parties argue back and forth in an attempt to fix blame, there is likely to be much more talking than listening going on. Arguing conclusions leads conflicting parties to focus on speaking instead of listening because parties are eager to correct each other's conclusions by stating their own.

THE PROBLEM WITH INFERENCES

One of the most robust findings in social psychological research is that of the fundamental attribution error (FAE). Basic attribution theory says that when we observe the behavior of others, we will try to understand, or make inferences about, why they have done what they've done. We decide whether the behavior resulted from something about the situation or something about the person's disposition or personality. The FAE refers to the tendency for people to underestimate the influence of the situation on a person's behavior. For example, if a coworker is late for an important meeting, you have the choice of explaining the behavior situationally (e.g., the person must have had some emergency) or dispositionally (e.g., the person is unprofessional). The FAE suggests that you will probably conclude that the person is unprofessional. We tend to make this error, however, only when we explain the behavior of *others,* not when we explain our own behavior. So if *you* are late for an important meeting, you will probably be able to offer up many situational factors that kept you from being on time (e.g., your alarm clock didn't work, the traffic was bad, the babysitter was sick).[35]

When we make dispositional inferences during conflicts, we are, more often than not, judging others negatively. Making negative judgments about others makes it less likely that we will be able to listen in the manner necessary to successfully work through conflict. In conflicts, the fundamental attribution error frequently occurs over intention. We often attribute the outcomes of a person's action or inaction to their intentions, when in fact this may not be the case. People wind up causing some sort of inconvenience or harm to another when they didn't intend to at all. That doesn't mean that the harm is any less damaging, but recognizing that it is not intentional is critical. It is a great deal easier to listen to someone who has harmed you when you don't think the person did it on purpose.

PREPARING TO LISTEN TO CONFLICT

In addition to avoiding the pitfalls outlined above, preparing to listen to conflict requires developing an attitude of curiosity, managing your emotions, and using reframing techniques.

AN ATTITUDE OF CURIOSITY

To listen effectively during conflicts, you have to be willing to listen to the other person's side of the story, even though you may completely disagree with it. This will be easier for you to do if you develop a genuine curiosity about the other person's perspective. We tend to enter into conflict conversations with the idea that we possess all the critical information relevant to the conflict. (After all, we know our side of things. What else could matter?) But there is always something we don't know, always more we can learn about the *other person's* perspective. Some small piece of information that the other person could share with us may change our understanding in some minor way—or perhaps entirely. How often have you been certain you were right about something or terribly angry with someone and then learned one small detail that changed things completely?

If we develop an attitude of curiosity, wherein we make our primary goal that of under-

Listen to This ▼

"Since feeling heard is often exactly what the aggrieved partner really is after, emotionally an act of empathy is a masterly tension reducer." [36]

—Daniel Goleman ▲

standing, we are more likely to listen to what the other party has to say. Understanding the other party is the first step toward conflict resolution, and that step is achieved through listening well.

Understanding the other party helps us in several ways. It gives us an idea of what it will take to resolve the conflict because we will have a better idea of the other party's needs. It creates trust. Our willingness to invest time and energy in listening to the other party communicates to that party that we are interested in working things out in a way that acknowledges the other party's interests. Finally, it increases the likelihood that the other party will listen to us. If we have been an attentive listener for the other party, he or she will feel more compelled to listen while giving us a turn to speak.

Listening well and understanding is not the same thing as agreeing. Even when you're listening effectively in a conflict conversation, you can certainly make your disagreements known. However, you do this after you've reached an understanding of the other party's views.

EMOTIONS

Conflict is inextricably tied to our emotions, but intense emotions can interfere with our ability to listen effectively, making it difficult to work through our conflicts. So what can we do? Our emotions often get the better of us during conflicts because the feelings we are experiencing are not directly addressed. Many people are uncomfortable talking about their feelings, particularly in a work-related environment. But we all know we don't check our feelings at the door when we show up at work. The people we work with are just as capable of making us laugh, cheering us up, wounding our pride, embarrassing us, and ticking us off as other people we know.

If we pretend that we don't experience feelings at work or decide they shouldn't be addressed, we set ourselves up to be sabotaged by our feelings later. While time is a great healer, feelings we try to ignore don't always just go away. They can make us blow up over something minor, or they can show up in more subtle, indirect ways, including the following:[37]

- **Judgments:** "If you were a team player, you would have been there for me."
- **Attributions:** "Why are you trying to ruin this project?"
- **Characterizations:** "You're too self-absorbed."
- **Problem solving:** "You need to change what you're doing."

The importance of dealing with your feelings is clear: You can't listen to another person if you're fuming inside. But feelings can be a complex web of emotions that require serious introspection to understand. Reflecting on your feelings can be the best way to anticipate and control your emotional reactions to a conflict. It can help you sort out what feelings are caused by the conflict itself and what feelings are caused by something else entirely.

Consider our example of Jane and Kelly, where Jane is feeling a threat to her identity of being smart because Kelly is arguing against one of Jane's ideas. Jane's emotional reaction to this conflict will be driven in part by her desire to have her idea supported and in part by the threat to her identity goal. This means that her emotional reaction might be quite intense and could be seen by others as inappropriate for the situation. Her overly intense emotional response will do two things: First, it will make it difficult for Jane to listen objectively to Kelly's ideas, and second, it will damage Jane's credibility, making it less likely that her coworkers will listen seriously to her.

Despite our best efforts at listening well during conflict, it is extremely easy to become wounded by an accusatory remark and slip into arguing. How can you listen without this happening? Remember to not let the conflict define who you are in that moment. It can help to imagine what the conflict will mean to you in three months or a year. Often, what seems horrible in the moment can seem incidental later on.

REFRAMING

It is difficult to maintain an attitude of curiosity and control over our emotions while we are being accused and blamed. One tool we can use as listeners is reframing. Reframing is a way of responding to a comment that changes its "frame," or subjective aspects, while maintaining its essential content. In essence, it is a way of reshaping the perceptions of the parties by changing negative language to more positive or neutral terms. In conflict, reframing can be used to keep the conflict from becoming destructive by taking the sting out of personal attacks or exaggerations. In addition, reframing can be used to help redefine what a conflict is about. Reframing can take the focus off personalities and redefine a conflict in terms of behaviors or the task at hand. Let's look at two examples of reframing.

> **A coworker says:** *I can't believe you brought this up to the client behind my back.*
> **Listener reframing feedback:** *Clearly you're upset that I spoke to the client without talking to you first.*

This feedback neutralizes this speaker's comment to some degree. "Behind my back" implies a sneakiness that isn't necessarily conveyed by "without talking to you first."

> **A team member says:** *You're a slacker and you're not pulling your weight around here.*
> **Listener reframing feedback:** *Perhaps you and I have different ideas about what I should be doing. I'd like to get a better understanding of your expectations.*

This feedback redefines the conflict. It changes the focus from a personal attack to differences in expectations.

Reframing can help us talk about feelings constructively during conflicts. We can listen for clues to the person's feelings, which we noted above are likely to be packaged as judgments, attributions, characterizations, and problem solving. When feelings are stated directly, they will often be delivered as "you" statements. (e.g., "You made me really mad.") "You" statements are problematic for two reasons: They are statements of blame, in that they make the listener responsible for the speaker's feelings. And they invite argument because the listener isn't likely to accept responsibility for how the other party feels. "I" statements get rid of the blame and offer nothing to argue about. For example, if someone says, "I was really mad," it's not likely that the listener will argue that, in actuality, the person wasn't mad.

When we are listening to "you" statements about a speaker's feelings, we can reframe comments so that the feelings are acknowledged and yet we are not accepting responsibility for them. ("I can see you're really angry about this.") Acknowledging the speaker's feelings is not the same thing as accepting blame for them. Even apologizing when a person is having a particular experience doesn't mean you are accepting responsibility for it.

We can listen for assumptions and inferences that are stated as "facts" and help the speaker reframe those as perceptions with our feedback. For example, a comment stated as a fact, such as "You have tried to squash this deal at every turn," can be reframed to a perception with "You're clearly unhappy with my input on this deal. Can we talk about the specifics?" You can also help them reframe sweeping generalizations that frequently begin with "always" or "never" to something more realistic.

> **Thought Box**
>
> 1. What is the most difficult part of listening to conflict for you? How comfortable are you discussing your feelings during a work-related conflict?
>
> 2. Have you allowed a business or personal relationship to deteriorate in order to avoid raising an issue with the other person? How could a listening approach to conflict have helped in this situation?

Reframing is not a technique to use with only the other party's comments. As you work through a conflict conversation, listen to yourself as well as to the other party. Pay attention to what you're thinking and saying as the conversation progresses, and reframe your thoughts and comments when necessary. That is, when you hear yourself thinking things like, "That is a really stupid thing to say" or "What an idiot," you can reframe those thoughts to something like, "I don't really understand why he's saying that" or "I disagree." This can help you maintain a listening mindset.

Listening through conflict requires time, energy, and commitment. It requires listening to what is being said—and for what is *not* being said. It requires checking the accuracy of your interpretations through questions and feedback. Because it is so demanding, it is not something to be undertaken when your relationship with the other party is temporary or of minimal importance. Listening through conflict is an investment in relationship building that should be made only when it's worth it. It is also best reserved for times when your listening energy is high, you have plenty of time, and you're in a comfortable physical and psychological environment.

Remember that your job is to listen and understand and to share your side when the other party is ready. Your job is not to make things right. If things are not going well, the best thing you can do is listen some more, but ultimately you may not be able to reach a mutually satisfying resolution.

LISTENING TO DEVELOP OTHERS

Can being listened to change a person's life? Thousands of nondirective psychologists and therapists believe it can and make their living from their efforts to do just that. Initially, it might seem like an exaggerated claim to suggest that listening has such power, but if we think about the fundamentals of personal growth and self-esteem, it doesn't seem unreasonable at all.

Human beings are social creatures. Our very sense of "self" and our understanding of how we fit into the world is a social construction. Anyone who has ever been around a newborn knows that people are born with a temperament, but from the moment of birth forward, our personality and view of ourselves are influenced by our interactions with others. When we interact with others, we see a reflection of ourselves in how they respond to us. Our parents or other primary caretakers reflect back to us our first sense of identity and position in the world. From parents gazing adoringly into the eyes of their newborn to praising their teenager for a job well done, these interactions all help to shape us into the people we become. Parents are by no means the only source of information about ourselves. Other important figures in our lives also shape us. Teachers, church leaders, extended family members, classmates, coworkers, and friends all contribute to our identity by reflecting back to us who they think we are.

The verbal and nonverbal messages that other people send us about ourselves are often pleasing, but not always. Parents may communicate that a child is the light of their life or an inconvenience; teachers may communicate that a student is intellectually impressive or annoyingly slow; teenagers may communicate that a peer is a leader or a loser. Unfortunately, negative messages from important others will influence one's sense of self just as the positive do.

Listening behavior is one way that communicators reflect back to each other perceptions of identity. When we listen to others nonjudgmentally, we affirm their self-worth and enhance their self-esteem. And when we listen to others with acceptance, we help them learn to accept themselves. Listening in this nonjudgmental and accepting way is one of the greatest gifts we can give a person of any age or background. Of course, we have all had conversations that haven't felt anything like receiving a gift. To harness the power of listening to develop and enable others, we must attempt the demanding and difficult undertaking of listening nonjudgmentally and with empathy.[38]

LISTENING NONJUDGMENTALLY

In our lifetime, most of us have experienced what it feels like to speak to someone who isn't really listening to us or who is listening with blame or judgment, and it's easy to interpret the person's poor listening as a reflection on us instead of them. We may feel we are not worthy, not good enough, or not valuable enough as a person to warrant being listened to well. It can feel like we aren't worth the other person's time or attention, like there isn't anything interesting or important about us.[39] While this is certainly unpleasant in any interaction, it has more serious consequences if it happens often and with important people in a person's life. If a person is regularly listened to with judgment and blame by important figures, low self-esteem and a poor self-image can result.

Even when unintended by the listener, poor listening or judgmental listening can feel like rejection to the speaker. For some speakers, this is experienced as a rejection of themselves as people rather than a rejection of what they are saying. Because rejection is unpleasant, many people suffer from some level of fear of rejection. They may hesitate to communicate openly with others because they are concerned that people will reject them. This manner of holding back can lead to serious social consequences because we build our relationships through communication. We come to know others and they come to know us through verbal and nonverbal exchange. Holding back communication can inhibit the growth of relationships and can ultimately lead to feelings of loneliness and isolation.[40]

Perhaps even worse than being listened to in this way by others is the tendency for people to impose judgmental listening upon themselves. Every day we are bombarded with images of ideals that are virtually unattainable, and because we are unable to achieve them we might feel guilty and blame ourselves. This often happens at a level below our conscious awareness. We don't know why we feel bad; we just know that we do. The feelings of guilt and blame can lead to low self-esteem, which surfaces in self-defeating behaviors. For example, some people reject all compliments, others don't take care of themselves (e.g., they eat too much or smoke), and others stay in abusive relationships.[41]

In contrast, really being listened to while self-disclosing or sharing ourselves helps us to create a sense of connection. It deepens our psychological intimacy with the listener. Being listened to in a nonjudgmental way communicates acceptance in a way that no other behavior can. Even claims of liking and caring will do little to make a person feel accepted if those claims are not accompanied by a willingness to listen. Nonjudgmental listening breaks through the psychological barriers of low self-esteem and fear of rejection that create social isolation. When listened to in a nonjudgmental way, people feel accepted and connected. Not only do they feel more accepted by others, they can also begin to feel more accepting of themselves. Just as poor or judgmental listening can negatively affect a speaker's self-image, good listening can positively affect it.[42]

LISTENING EMPATHICALLY

Listening nonjudgmentally is challenging. It requires us, for those moments we're listening, to cease to impose our view of the world onto the speaker's story. Ordinarily when we listen to others, we evaluate what they are saying according to our own attitudes, values, and beliefs. As someone speaks, we might be thinking, "I wouldn't have done it that way," or "That wasn't very smart thinking," or "How could you not know that would happen?" To listen in a way that affirms another person and makes them feel truly connected, we have to listen empathically.

Empathic listening goes beyond merely understanding what is being said. It goes beyond giving feedback and asking perception-checking questions. Although it includes these, it also requires us to step out of our own world for the moment and enter the world of the speaker. In essence, we aren't just trying to understand how the speaker sees things, we are attempting to take on the speaker's perspective, see things through his or her eyes, and grasp the speaker's underlying feelings.[43] Stepping out of our own world and stepping into the perspective of another is a sacrifice we make in order to listen empathically. During the time that you are listening empathically, you sacrifice your own point of view and your own perspective, which is difficult to do.

Of course, entering the world of the other doesn't mean that you necessarily agree with it, only that you can relate to the person's perspective. Consider this situation. Imagine that a friend has revealed to you that for some time he has been aware of the criminal activity of a colleague. He has avoided coming forward with the information because of his fear of some negative reprisal. In your opinion, the fear is unfounded because the colleague is at the same level in the organization, not a higher-up. Furthermore, you think coming forward is simply the right thing to do. If you respond to your friend by saying that the threat really isn't that serious and that he should do the right thing by coming forward, you are listening judgmentally. If your goal is to listen empathically, you have to be able to see how, to him, the threat is very real and how he feels that he is in a situation where he has no choice.

Listening empathically doesn't mean that you agree with what is said, nor does it mean that you are unable to offer your thoughts or suggestions to the speaker. But be careful of your goal before you do. If your goal is simply to be an empathic listener, your thoughts and suggestions

Listen to This ▼

"Real communication occurs, and this evaluative tendency is avoided, when we listen with understanding. What does this mean? It means to see the expressed idea and attitude from the other person's point of view, to sense how it feels to him, to achieve his frame of reference in regard to the thing he is talking about." [44]

—Carl Rogers ▲

are not going to get you there. Furthermore, if you are attempting to communicate acceptance, sharing your thoughts and suggestions may communicate that the person isn't doing something right or isn't capable of producing a solution to the problem. If you must communicate your thoughts and suggestions, consider doing so at another time. Listen first, talk later.

Despite our best intentions and sincere effort, we will never be able to completely take on another person's perspective. After all, a person's view results from his or her unique experience in the world. All we will ever have is our view of the speaker's perspective. However, that is one step closer to true empathy than judging the speaker's message from only our own point of view.

According to Carl Rogers and Richard Farson, there are definite "dos" and "don'ts" of this type of listening.[45]

What to Avoid

Avoid trying to get the other person to see things from your perspective. Really, you're just trying to understand the other person's perspective.

Avoid offering demanding feedback. Often, listeners respond with questions that demand the speaker to make a decision; to either agree or disagree. This is usually just another way that listeners try to get speakers to change their perspective, see the error of their ways, and come to view things as the listener does.

Avoid passing judgment or offering advice. Both of these make it difficult to create a safe climate for exploration by the speaker. Even positive evaluations by the listener can influence the speaker and impede the exploration process.

What to Do

Listen and respond to the total meaning of a message. Understanding both the words a person says and the feelings behind them is important for active listening. Getting the words, but not the feelings, can actually damage a relationship. Sometimes communicating feelings is the true objective of the speaker. The actual word content could be meaningless or absurd without the feelings.

Attend to both verbal and nonverbal cues. Much of the emotion expressed by an individual is through nonverbal communication. Tone of voice, hesitancies when speaking, facial expressions, posture, and other nonverbal cues help to communicate the feelings behind the words. For some people, feelings are rarely, if ever, openly stated.

Have the right attitude. Remaining nonjudgmental when listening represents a major attitude shift for most of us. Developing a sincere interest in the speaker can help us make this shift and also make us appear sincere to the speaker. Speakers can usually recognize a listener who is only applying a listening technique or simply going through the motions of empathic listening without having any genuine interest in what is being said. Either the speaker will recognize the lack of true interest, or he or she will sense that something is off about the listener and may not trust him or her. This idea points again to the fact that active listening is an investment for the listener and isn't desirable or appropriate in all circumstances.

Listening at this level is a demanding task for anyone and requires immense energy and focus. Katie Graham-Holan is licensed psychotherapist who spends about 80 percent of her workday listening deeply to clients. At most, she sees six clients per day for 50 minutes each. "It's not humanly possible for me to see more than that," she explains. "I'm not just listening to the words that come out of their mouth. I'm observing everything." That sort of attention requires a commitment to staying focused on what the other person is trying to communicate

---

Thought Box

1. To whom do you go when you need someone to listen to you? What does this person do that makes him or her a good person to talk to?

2. What do you find most difficult about listening empathically? Is it easier to listen empathically to some people more than others? Is there someone you need to listen to empathically but with whom you are unable to achieve listening at this level? What can you do to improve your listening in this situation?

3. As an employee, have you been listened to empathically? What effect did it have on you?

---

and not drifting off in thought. "I have a strong intention to be present when I see someone. It requires a lot of energy because our natural human tendency is to turn things back to ourselves. I really believe it requires that intention to be present and that is one of the most generous gifts you can give someone." Because she recognizes the challenge associated with listening at this level, Graham-Holan works at being sure she's up to the task. She eats right, exercises, and gets enough sleep. To improve one's skill at listening deeply, Graham-Holan recommends any kind of practice at cultivating focus, such as meditation or yoga, and working at clearing away personal filters in listening, such as getting to know oneself. "The more connected you are with yourself, the more authentic you can be with person you're with and the more you can connect with them." Ultimately, she says, "Take care of your total self so you can be present."[46]

In this textbook, we have argued that listening should be goal oriented and that strategic listening should be employed to enhance the likelihood of accomplishing our listening objective. In this chapter, we discussed tactics for improving listening effectiveness in specific listening situations: listening to learn, listening to persuasive messages, listening to conflict, and listening to develop others. For managers, each of these listening situations will doubtlessly be encountered with fair regularity. In the next chapter, we offer managers ways to use the concept of listening at the organizational level to improve business outcomes and solve business problems.

DISCUSSION QUESTIONS

1. With a group, listen to a Rush Limbaugh or Laura Ingraham show, or watch the *NBC Nightly News*. Is the information presented in an unbiased manner? What techniques are used to bias the information?

2. Is propaganda ethical? What is the difference between ethical and unethical persuasion? What reaction do you think people have when they hear unethical persuasion attempts? Why are these attempts so common?

3. How does interpersonal conflict affect the workplace? Do most workplace conflicts simply go away over time? What are the consequences of unaddressed conflicts that don't just go away?

4. What effect does stress in the workplace have on a person's ability to listen to conflict?

5. In what situations would a manager want to engage in empathic listening? In what situations would this be inappropriate?

ENDNOTES

1. C. Coakley and A. Wolvin, "Listening in the Educational Environment," in M. Purdy and D. Borisoff (eds.), *Listening in Everyday Life,* 2nd ed. (Lanham, MD: University Press of America, 1997), 179–212.

2. A. Wolvin and C. Coakley, *Listening,* 5th ed. (Boston: McGraw Hill, 1996).

3. Adapted from J. D. Bransford and M. K. Johnson, "Contextual Prerequisites for Understanding: Some Investigations of Comprehension and Recall," *Journal of Verbal Learning and Verbal Behavior* 717 (1972): 717–726.

4. "International Listening Association." Retrieved September 20, 2004, from http://www.listen.org.

5. Wolvin and Coakley, *supra* n. 2.

6. Wolvin and Coakley, *supra* n. 2.

7. "Francis Bacon Quotes." Retrieved June 25, 2004, from http://www.brainyquote.com/quotes/authors/f/francis_bacon.html.

8. P. Hunsaker and A. Alessandra, *The Art of Managing People* (New York: Simon & Schuster, 1980).

9. R. E. Petty and John T. Cacioppo, "The Elaboration Likelihood Model of Persuasion," in L. Berkowitz, *Advances in Experimental Social Psychology,* vol. 19 (San Diego: Academic Press, 1986).

10. Ibid.

11. Shaw, "George Bernard Shaw Quotes." Retrieved June 25, 2004, from http://www.brainyquote.com/quotes/authors/g/george_bernard_shaw.html.

12. A. H. Eagley and S. Chaiken, *The Psychology of Attitudes* (Fort Worth: Harcourt Brace Jovanovich College Publishers, 1993).

13. Ibid.

14. Ibid.

15. "William James Quotes." Retrieved June 25, 2004, from http://www.brainyquote.com/quotes/authors/w/william_james.html.

16. R. Matlon, "Propositions of Fact," in *Debating Propositions of Value: An Idea Revisited,* Cross Examination Debate Association Yearbook, vol. 9, 1988. Available at http://debate.uvm.edu/NFL/rostrumlib/propfactmatlon1294.pdf.

17. H. Simons, J. Morreale, and B. Gronbeck, *Persuasion in Society* (Thousand Oaks, CA: Sage Publishing, 2001).

18. W. Booth, G. Colomb, and J. Williams, *The Craft of Research* (Chicago: University of Chicago Press, 1995).

19. "Franklin D. Roosevelt Quotes." Retrieved June 25, 2004, from http://www.brainyquote.com/quotes/authors/f/franklin_d_roosevelt.html.

20. Booth et al., *supra* n. 18.

21. H. Gardner, *Changing Minds* (Boston: Harvard Business School Press, 2004), 126.

22. "Propaganda Critic: About This Site." Retrieved September 29, 2002, from http://www.propagandacritic.com/articles/about.html.

23. "Propaganda Critic: Examples. Enron." Retrieved March 29, 2004, from http://www.propagandacritic.com/articles/examples.enron.html.

24. R. E. Riggio and H. S. Friedman, "Individual Differences in Cues to Deception," *Journal of Personality and Social Psychology* 45 (1983): 889–915.

25. "International Listening Association." Retrieved January 12, 2004, from http://www.listen.org.

26. R. Gass and J. Seiter, *Persuasion, Social Influence, and Compliance Gaining,* 2nd ed. (Needham Heights, MA: Allyn & Bacon, 2003).
27. Ibid.
28. M. Wheeler, "True or False? Lie Detection at the Bargaining Table," *Negotiation* 1, no. 1 (2003).
29. Gass and Seiter, *supra* n. 26, 259–281.
30. "William James Quotes." Retrieved June 25, 2004, from http://www.brainyquote.com/quotes/ authors/w/william_james.html.
31. D. Stone, B. Patton, and S. Heen, *Difficult Conversations* (New York: Penguin Books, 2000).
32. D. Goleman. *Emotional Intelligence* (New York: Bantam Books, 1995), 60.
33. Stone, Patton, and Heen, *supra* n. 31.
34. Ibid., 36.
35. L. Ross and R. E. Nisbett, *The Person and the Situation: Perspectives in Social Psychology* (Philadelphia: Temple University Press, 1991).
36. D. Goleman, *Emotional Intelligence* (New York: Bantam Books, 1995).
37. Stone, Patton, and Heen, *supra* n. 31.
38. J. E. Sullivan, *The Good Listener* (Notre Dame, IN: Ave Maria Press, 2000).
39. Ibid.
40. Ibid.
41. Ibid.
42. Ibid.
43. Ibid.
44. C. R. Rogers and F. J. Roethlisberger, "Barriers and Gateways to Communication," *Harvard Business Review* 30, no. 4 (1952): 47.
45. C. R. Rogers and R. E. Farson, "Active Listening," in R. G. Newman, M. A. Danziger, and M. Cohen (eds.), *Communication in Business Today* (Boston: D.C. Heath & Company, 1987). Excerpt available at http://www.centerfortheperson.org/10.html.
46. K. Graham-Holan, personal interview, April 2004.

4 THE LISTENING ORGANIZATION

W hat is a listening organization, and what effect does being a listening organization have on business outcomes? To answer that question, consider the example of the Panera Bread Company. Panera Bread began as the Au Bon Pain Company in 1981. Between 1993 and 1997, a new brand concept was developed, and in 1999 the company name was changed to Panera Bread. Since that time, the value of the company's stock has grown thirteenfold, and the company has been recognized as one of *Business Week*'s "100 Hot Growth Companies."[1] Its phenomenal growth results in large part from the company's willingness to listen and respond to customers.

Ron Shaich, the chairman and CEO of Panera Bread, spends a great deal of his time in more than 750 Panera Bread stores, asking his customers questions and learning from their answers. He then leads the company in directions that respond to what he's learned. Shaich faced a challenging moment with the popularity of the Atkins diet, which discourages consumption of starchy foods such as bread. He learned through focus groups that his customers were paying increasing attention to their intake of carbohydrates, sugar, and fat grams.[2] Panera Bread responded by developing a variety of lower-carb offerings, including Italian herb bread and an Asiago cheese bagel. Since then, Shaich has continued to push for adapting and improving the menu in ways that demonstrate his commitment to understanding the company's customers and meeting their needs. He says, "We will continue to evolve with our customers and serve them in any way we can."[3] Bearing this out, most stores have free Wi-Fi access. According to Shaich, "Panera bread is the first national chain to take substantial steps forward in meeting growing consumer demand for high-speed Internet access without charging for the service."[4]

Organizations have a variety of sources to listen to, both internal and external. Various "speakers" are able to provide organizations with insights critical to growth and, ultimately, survival. The internal voices of employees can teach organizations how to improve morale, raise productivity, and reduce turnover. External speakers, including customers, suppliers, shareholders, and others, can provide organizations with insights they may not be able to uncover on their own. Some companies, such as Panera Bread, recognize the value of listening and responding to these sources, and others don't.

A culture of listening can be difficult to develop, but organizations that don't foster this sort of environment can pay a heavy price. Both the *Challenger* and *Columbia* disasters have been attributed, in part, to an organizational culture that didn't want to listen.[5] The National Aero-

"Last Saturday [February 1, 2003], as I was working on my computer here in East Texas, I heard a very powerful rumbling sound that shook our house. It was thirty minutes later that I discovered it was the Columbia *breaking apart overhead. As soon as I learned the tragic news my thoughts flashed back to the first shuttle disaster and I wondered if not listening to warning had brought about this disaster as well."* [7]

—J. Howard Baker ▲

nautics and Space Administration (NASA) became a victim of its own perfection. In the 1960s, NASA achieved remarkable success, accomplishing the seemingly impossible goal of sending men to the moon. After this success, there was pressure to maintain the unstoppable "can-do" culture, but this backfired by creating an environment that discouraged dissent and in which negative information was not listened to. The report released by the Columbia Accident Investigation Board stated, "The NASA organizational culture had as much to do with this accident as the foam."[6]

Many factors can contribute to creating a culture of listening, including the physical facility, available resources, procedures, and policies. Office cubicles may invite distraction, uncomfortable workspaces create stress, and the arrangement of offices and break areas may discourage interaction. Limited resources can have an impact by creating conflict. Procedures and policies—or lack thereof—can convey a closed communication climate. Even the décor of offices can create a cold and impersonal environment and have an impact on whether effective listening is fostered or inhibited.

The most important factor by far, however, is leadership. Company leaders have a direct effect on the culture as well as an indirect effect through their influence over the other factors that contribute to culture. Managers, for example, can create a closed communication culture by displaying a "kill the messenger" attitude. It's natural for managers to be upset when they receive bad news. When something isn't working well in the manager's unit, the failure will reflect poorly on him or her. But when managers react emotionally to bad news, they may discourage others from bringing negative messages to them in the future. The bad news will still be there; the managers just won't hear about it. Similarly, if managers respond to messages in a disrespectful or discourteous way—or alternatively, if they don't respond at all—people will be less inclined to bring information to them. A nonlistening climate will also be fostered when midlevel managers feel threatened by employee ideas or suggestions. Managers may feel that the employee is suggesting something that they themselves should have thought of. Senior management can help prevent this by encouraging managers to seek employee input and reward them for obtaining employee participation in submitting suggestions.

In the same way as managers can contribute to the creation of a closed communication climate, when such a climate exists it is up to management to open it up. An important first step in turning around a closed, nonlistening culture is building trust. In a situation with inequity in power, the party with the least power will evaluate how much information can be safely shared. The more trust, the more sharing. To create a listening culture, leaders have to ensure that people know they can report bad news or dissenting opinions and not somehow be punished for them. Managers have to encourage employees to feel secure about sharing information without fear that the information will be used to harm them through embarrassment, criticism, career damage, humiliation, or other means.

An analysis of the system of communication as a whole can provide managers with innovative possibilities for creating change in a closed communication culture. A simple change to any element in the communication system can have a sweeping effect on the entire communication process. For example, if mistrust exists between employees and management or among various departments, building a bridge of trust might be facilitated by a change in communication context. Perhaps people habitually think and behave in a particular way when they are in their normal work settings. Changing the backdrop can often help bring about change in the dialogue. General Electric's Jack Welch realized this when he instituted his "Work-Out" teams in 1988. The Work-Out teams were interdepartmental groups that met outside their ordinary work environments. They analyzed problems from the varying perspectives and offered recommendations for reducing inefficiencies. Currently, GE's Work-Out teams continue to increase employee involvement in guiding change for the company and may sometimes include customers or suppliers when applicable.[8]

DETERMINING HOW WELL YOUR ORGANIZATION LISTENS

Although a number of conditions can affect the success of an organization, the very survival of any organization depends on how well information is gathered, shared, and stored. One way to diagnose the effectiveness of listening in your organization is through a communication audit. A communication audit analyzes the organization's internal and/or external communication with the goal of mapping out the current communication situation, including the communication policies, practices, strengths, and weaknesses. The audit is designed to provide management with information that can be used to make decisions on how to improve communication.

Innumerable possibilities exist for the focus of an audit. Communication audits can be general and exploratory in nature or designed to target a specific problem. An exploratory audit might serve to confirm a manager's expectations about communication in the company or bring to the manager's awareness areas of concern. For example, the owner of a dry cleaning business learned from an audit of external communication that his customers were unaware of his specialty services. He thought he had communicated those offerings quite well but learned that his messages had not been effective.

An audit that focuses on specific issues might investigate a broad area, such as how employees use communication technologies or how a particular procedure affects the flow of communication. Alternatively, the focus could be on a fairly narrow issue, such as whether a particular message is attended to and understood. Most audits involve plotting communication networks and checking the quality of communication relationships. A well-done audit relates communication to organizational outcomes and makes recommendations.

A communication audit offers a number of benefits. First, management can develop a better understanding of successful and unsuccessful communication within the organization. Sometimes employees fail to understand messages or assume they know something they don't actually know. A communication audit can reveal those issues before they develop into serious problems for the organization. A communication audit also demonstrates to all employees in the organization that they are valued and are contributors to defining and solving problems. Furthermore, a communication audit sensitizes people within the organization to the communication process. Simply possessing a heightened awareness of the process can improve how employees communicate.[9]

So who should conduct a communication audit? It is usually advisable to arrange for someone outside the organization, or at least a person with no vested interest in the focal issue, to complete the audit. This is true for several reasons. First, managers often have an understandably distorted view of the organization, which can lead to a bias in the collection, analysis, and interpretation of the data collected through an audit. Furthermore, an effective audit requires an openness to the unexpected. This can be difficult for managers to maintain, especially if the analysis uncovers something unpleasant.

Several methods are available for conducting communication audits, including observation, content analysis of communication samples, and communication diaries. The two most common techniques are interviews and questionnaires. Interviews offer the advantages of greater disclosure because people are inclined to say more than they will write. A limitation of the interview is that the data are more difficult to summarize and analyze than the responses on a questionnaire. A typical analysis audit involves analyzing transcripts or summaries of interviews for emerging themes. Questionnaires generate less disclosure and offer no opportunity for the auditor to ask probing follow-up questions, but the data collected are usually easy to analyze quantitatively.

A well-conducted communication audit can be a useful tool to help managers gain a better understanding of communication within the organization at a particular point in time. Of particular interest for our purposes is the insight into the listening effectiveness of the organization that an audit can reveal. An audit focusing on listening could reveal missed messages, misunderstandings and misperceptions, lack of responsiveness to messages, bottlenecks and stoppages in the flow of information, and low levels of satisfaction with the organization's listening practices among employees or external stakeholders. Of course, an audit can also reveal what organizations are doing right.

Communication audits can provide a snapshot of an organization's communication and help in assessing organizational listening. Creating a culture of listening, however, doesn't occur as a result of an audit alone. A culture of listening is the result of the modeling of effective listening by company leaders and the application of effective listening techniques. In this chapter, we discuss listening opportunities for organizations and explore techniques for listening effectively at the organizational level.

LISTENING TO LEARN FROM EMPLOYEES

Organizations have a marvelous opportunity to learn by listening to employees. Employees often have ideas about how the organization can improve its processes and procedures, better serve its customers, and, of course, motivate and satisfy workers. The Employee Involvement Association (formerly the National Association of Suggestion Systems) estimates that organizations with suggestion programs save between $28,000 and $48,000 per 100 employees per year.[10] Douglas Battery Manufacturing Company was able to reduce back injury claims by 40 percent within a single year thanks to employee suggestions. Monarch Marking System of Ohio was able to cut the space needed for an assembly area by 70 percent and reduce late shipments by an astounding 90 percent

Listen to This ▼

"Management doesn't listen to workers unless there is a structured system." [11]

—Roy Baum

President, Employee Involvement Association ▲

by implementing employee suggestions. Intel's first microprocessor and 3M's Post-it Notes both began with employee suggestions.[12]

Still, only about 3 percent of organizations have formal employee suggestion programs, and many of those are not very effective.[13] Ailing suggestion systems suffer from two main problems: Employees don't feel they get satisfactory responses to their suggestions, and they don't feel adequately rewarded for their participation.

In cases where suggestions or complaints from employees don't get much of a response, a suggestion might be dropped in the box and the employee never hears anything in reply, or the employee receives a polite letter rejecting the suggestion without any further explanation. Participants in focus group research on suggestion boxes in organizations complained, "It's like dropping something into the black hole." One employee from a manufacturing facility said that she had been dropping the same note into her company's box for the past year. The note simply asks, "Does anyone read these suggestions?" She has yet to receive a reply.[14]

If a suggestion box is set up, managers must realize that employees who submit a suggestion eagerly await a response. If they don't get one, if it comes too late, or if it is a form letter with an unsatisfactory reply, the suggestion box can actually end up increasing the feeling of disconnectedness that employees have with management. To manage employee expectations and to encourage management to respond in a timely fashion, it can be helpful to establish a time frame in which employees can expect feedback (e.g., within 48 hours or one week of submission).

Sometimes the reason a suggestion goes unacknowledged is that a single human resources person is responsible for handling all the suggestions that come in. In today's work environment, with everyone trying to do more in less time, it's not surprising that suggestions sometimes receive little attention. As one human resources manager admits, "I just count the number of suggestions. I don't have time to read them anymore." One way to overcome this problem is to do something similar to what the Florida Department of Revenue did when it implemented its program called "Listening to You." The program requires *supervisors* to respond to suggestions, questions, and complaints of employees rather than a lone representative from human resources.[15]

In a further effort to curb the "blowoff" response, the organization assigns the suggestions or complaints to supervisors by rotation, not by supervisory area. This means that often, in order to respond, a supervisor must research an issue to find out whether a suggestion will work or how a complaint can be resolved. To prepare for the program, supervisors all receive training in listening and in solving problems. As a tribute to its success, the level of participation in the program doubled in the first few years.[16]

Employees also complain that they are not rewarded for their suggestions. To address this problem, some organizations pay employees for suggestions that are used, but this can backfire. Employees may submit similar ideas, and if one idea is selected and the other is not, the unrewarded employee can feel resentful. Some employees actually think that

Listen to This ▼

"Good suggestions can come from all levels of the organization, and employees who interact regularly with clients or vendors can offer especially valuable feedback for improving products and services." [17]

—Diane Domeyer
Executive Director, OfficeTeam ▲

Thought Box

How does your current organization or school do at internal listening? What feedback opportunities exist in your current organization or school? Do you feel that those opportunities are adequate? What recommendations would you make to improve the process?

---

managers make small changes to suggestions before implementing them so that the company won't have to pay a reward. Furthermore, monetary reward systems pit employees against one another. This can inhibit the flow of conversation and the development of ideas among employees. Employees may be reluctant to sit around the break room, discussing ideas for improvements with one another, when they could submit the ideas individually for a financial reward. As a result, discussions that stimulate thinking and inspire innovation may be restrained.[18]

Listening to employees can help organizations improve their productivity, safety record, employee retention, and ultimately, their bottom line. But employees will be hesitant to deliver information if they are concerned about how it will be received. Employees have to know that they will be listened to in an open and nonthreatening way in order to bring suggestions, complaints, or other information to the attention of managers.

DEVELOPING EMPLOYEES THROUGH LISTENING

Listening openly to employee suggestions and complaints is a way of learning how to improve the organization. But listening empathically, connecting with employees, and building employees' self-esteem through listening offers other benefits to the organization. Listening empathically to employees can lead to numerous positive outcomes:

1. **Listening to employees builds stronger relationships with them.** Connections are formed and relationships are developed through communication. Those bonds are weak, however, if communication flows in only one direction. Each time an employee leaves an organization, it costs the company about one-third the beginning salary for the position to hire a replacement. This provides smart managers with plenty of motivation to retain good employees when possible. Building strong connections with employees helps reduce turnover.[19] When employees feel that someone cares about what they have to say, they will perceive a confirmation of their value to the organization.

2. **Listening to employees can lead to their growth as workers and increase their feelings of confidence about their place within the organization.** Employees may not automatically open up their communication to managers and initially may need to be asked

---

Listen to This ▼

"Outstanding leaders go out of their way to boost the self-esteem of their personnel. If people believe in themselves, it's amazing what they can accomplish."[20]
—Sam Walton ▲

open-ended questions to encourage them to communicate openly. People who are listened to feel better about themselves. Employees can become more confident in themselves and feel empowered if their managers listen to them. They are more likely to think creatively, produce ideas, and act like self-starters.

3. **Listening to employees can help them work through issues affecting their performance.** Or you can find out what is affecting their work. Often we try to change employees by prescribing what needs to be done or how the person should change. These direct efforts will most often fail because people typically become defensive when others try to change them. People respond this way in part because criticism is simply no fun to hear. But often, more is going on. Many psychologists believe people always have some known—or unknown—practical reason for their behavior. Even behaviors that appear self-defeating and counterproductive serve some sort of function for the individual engaging in them. Telling someone to change a behavior is often unsuccessful because the function served by that behavior is being ignored. Through listening, managers are more likely to understand what is really going on with an employee and produce a more effective way of shaping the employee's behavior.

Listen to This ▼

"Most people don't care what you know until they know that you care." [21]
—Muffet McGraw
Head Coach, Women's Basketball,
University of Notre Dame ▲

An important question for most managers, however, is, "How do these benefits affect business outcomes? Are there measurable advantages to the organization related to these benefits?" Actually, there are.

In their book *First Break All the Rules,* Marcus Buckingham and Curt Coffman describe the wisdom revealed through more than 25 years of qualitative and quantitative data collection by the Gallup researchers.[22] The Gallup Organization has studied productive organizations and individuals for more than a quarter of a century, and Buckingham and Coffman detail the findings of this research in their book. The study shows the relationship between employee perceptions and business outcomes. Specifically, a relationship was discovered between how employees answered 12 questions and the organizational results along four business outcomes: productivity, profitability, retention, and customer satisfaction. Of the 12 questions, six were most strongly associated with better business outcomes. Four of those six questions are relevant here:

1. Do I have the materials and equipment I need to do my work right?
2. At work, do I have the opportunity to do what I do best every day?
3. Does my supervisor, or someone at work, seem to care about me as a person?
4. Is there someone at work who encourages my development?

It is easy to see how these questions are related to listening. Questions 1 and 2 have to do with listening to employees well enough to know whether they believe they have what they need to do their job and whether their job allows them to work in their strongest areas. Through their analysis of thousands of interviews, Buckingham and Coffman discovered that great managers tend to avoid trying to change employees to fit a job. Instead, they try to draw out from employees their natural talents and match those abilities to a need in the organization. Then they attempt to give the employees what they need to be successful.

> **Thought Box**
>
> At what companies in your work experience were you able to grow and develop? What contributed to that growth? Have you ever worked in an environment where you felt judged or unappreciated? What contributed to that feeling? How did it affect your performance?

Questions 3 and 4 have to do with listening empathically. We let employees know that we care about them as human beings through listening to them and showing an interest in what they say. As one of the managers interviewed by Gallup said when talking about one of his best teams, "I spent a lot of time with them. I listened. I took them out for dinner, had a couple of drinks with them. Had them over to my place for holidays. But mostly I was just interested in who they were."[23] The authors recommend spending time talking to employees within a week or two of hiring and then periodically during their employment to learn the employees' perspective on their strengths, weaknesses, goals, and how they think things are going. Of course, the answers to these questions will be based on the perceptions of the employees, not some objective reality, so managers may not agree with the answers that the employees give. But for these questions, it's the employees' thoughts that matter.

Sometimes employees just need someone to talk to when they are going through difficult times, even if those difficulties have little to do with work. Over the past 15 years, the responsibility for listening to employee woes has shifted from human resources and personnel departments to direct supervisors and line managers. Some companies train their managers to prepare them for this often stressful sort of interaction. In addition, they may create alternative outlets for their employees to turn to. Lyreco, an office stationery and supply company, trains managers in listening and counseling as part of its leadership program. The company also provides access to advice lines for help with debt or employment-related legal issues to meet the diverse needs of employees wanting a listening ear. Other companies have established Internet or intranet forums for employees to communicate their concerns. Some organizations, such as Glaxo-SmithKline and Parker Pens, have a workplace chaplain available at some of their locations.[24]

One final finding of the Gallup research is that managers are more important than organizations when it comes to the relationship between employee perceptions and business outcomes. Even if employees don't feel supported by an organization, they can still feel supported by their immediate manager, and the relationship to the business outcomes holds. The message here is that middle managers make the difference. Even if your company couldn't be considered a listening organization, you can reap the business rewards in your department by being a listening manager.

LISTENING TO LEARN FROM CUSTOMERS

After owning his brand-new Ford for a mere eight months, Russell White was on his third trip to the car dealer's repair shop. As he sat in the shop's waiting area, he made a comment to the owner of the dealership that he wasn't too happy about having to be there yet again. The owner responded with, "Well, having a car in here three times in eight months for minor repairs isn't all that bad." This response was so inappropriate that it prompted White to write a letter to the Ford corporate offices in Dearborn, telling about his experience with his car. His letter received a quick and impressive reply. Ford told White it was deeply concerned about the problems with his car. Through several more contacts, Ford informed White that after researching the problem, it was initiating a recall on the part that had continually failed in his car. [25]

For White, the listening he experienced while face to face with the dealership owner was ineffective at best and could have damaged his relationship with Ford. With most customers, it would have been left at that. White's family, friends, and coworkers might have heard (perhaps repeatedly) about his frustrations with his car, but Ford wouldn't have heard about it. And the next time he needed a new car, White probably would have avoided Ford dealers. But because he took the time to write a letter, Ford's reputation with White was salvaged, and an important problem for the company was brought to light. If the dealership owner had been a better listener, Ford would have reaped these benefits without White's writing the letter, and White's opinion of the dealership owner would be better than it most likely is.

The point of this story is that at one level, the corporate level, Ford was listening and responding well. At another level, the "front lines," the listening was poor. In any industry, if you trace the path of a product from raw materials to end user, the customers involved and the opportunities for listening are many. However, the unfortunate truth is that, unlike White, most customers who have a complaint don't take the time to write a letter. Despite the many opportunities for feedback, spontaneous feedback from customers is most likely to occur in the front lines, where customers interact with sellers. For manufacturers and the corporate offices of service providers, this means being cut out of the direct, spontaneous feedback loop, and they have to work, sometimes hard, to get customer feedback.

Though most of us don't really enjoy listening to people complain, feedback from customers often appears in the form of a complaint. Organizations should welcome complaints as free informational gifts from customers. Of course, organizations can benefit greatly from listening to customers about more than only their grievances and from listening to customers who would be unlikely to actually submit a complaint. This, however, can be a daunting task, requiring planning and effort.

USING SURVEYS

A common approach for listening to customers is survey research. Surveys offer some distinct advantages over other methods of seeking customer input. They are fairly inexpensive to perform, they can easily reach many people distributed over large areas because they can be conducted by mail or by phone, and they yield quantitative data, which is easy to analyze. Still, the use of surveys should be limited to easy questions about behaviors ("How many times a week do you go to the supermarket?") or attitudes ("Which is your preferred brand of shampoo?").

One limitation of surveys lies in the way the questions are usually constructed. Most surveys are questionnaires with structured questions—and structured responses. These multiple-choice surveys restrict the respondent to choosing an answer from a set of alternatives. Few surveys contain open-ended questions that allow customers to choose the direction of their answers.

Structured responses may make the data easier to summarize and analyze, but the problem with them is that only responses known to the ones creating the survey are offered to the respondents, and thus, only responses that are already known to the organization will be *given* by the respondents. So customers are not able to introduce any new ideas or complaints—quite simply,

"Whether you're marketing products and services for a billion-dollar corporation or are out peddling a start-up brand, you can find more to say, and can do a better job of selling, once you listen to your customer." [26]

—Bonnie Goebert

Marketing research consultant ▲

they aren't able to reveal anything to the organization of which it is not already aware. For example, Barbara recently completed a telephone survey about the radio stations she listens to. For each question, she was offered five alternatives from which to select her answer. For several of the questions, her answer didn't match any of the options. The surveyor on the other end of the line pushed her toward a selection despite her protests that the answer wasn't exactly right. How much deep listening is an organization doing if it is providing the answers to its own questions and forcing respondents to choose among them?

USING FOCUS GROUPS

One way to alleviate the problem of structured responses is to listen to customers through focus groups. A focus group is a marketing research technique in which a gathering of consumers is led into a discussion by a moderator. The group discussion is analyzed using qualitative techniques to reveal ideas and themes. Surveys may tell organizations how customers respond in a given way to a question, but a focus group will help organizations understand *why* customers respond as they do.

Bonnie Goebert, head of a research consulting firm in New York with more than 30 years of experience with focus groups and coauthor of *Beyond Listening: Learning the Secret Language of Focus Groups,* suggests that this method works best for five basic purposes:[27]

1. **To explore customers' habits.** Gevalia Kaffe, a Swedish mail-order brand, hired Goebert to study consumer behavior. At that time, when customers became Gevalia subscribers, they received a "starter kit" that contained a promotional newsletter about the coffee plant and several brochures about Sweden. Goebert found that when the customers received the kits, they threw aside all the written material, never reading any of it. With this information, Gevalia was able to refocus its efforts to more productive means of promotion.

2. **To learn more about consumer attitudes.** Betty Crocker created a one-step (just add liquid) cake mix in the 1950s. It thought the product, which would make a woman's life easier, would be a certain success. It was wrong. As it turns out, Betty Crocker made it a little *too* easy. Women didn't feel good about making a cake that required so little from them, so the chefs at Betty Crocker changed the product so that it required adding water and an egg, and that did the trick.

3. **To examine a brand's image.** When Nestea came out with a fresh-brewed tea to be sold as a premium tea in the refrigerator section, competing with Snapple and similar brands, it learned through listening to consumers that it had a lot of work to do. The Nestea brand had an image of being quick, not-so-great-tasting liquid that wasn't really even in the tea category in the minds of customers.

4. **To discern consumer's emotional bonds with a product.** The makers of Pine-Sol thought that customers were emotionally connected to the hazing action that occurs when the product is added to water. It took Pine-Sol listening to its customers to realize that customers were actually emotionally attached to the strong pine scent and to the memories of that smell from childhood.

5. **To develop an effective advertising campaign.** In one study, the makers of Excedrin were considering what label to use for an Excedrin ibuprofen product. What Excedrin found was that the brand had an image as a headache medicine. Its next advertising campaign focused on Excedrin as the tough headache medicine.

Goebert offers listening points for dealing with focus groups. She recommends asking probing questions but being cautious about steering group members toward specific answers. The questions should avoid suggesting the "correct" answer to the respondents. She also recommends listening to verbal and nonverbal cues and even paying attention to silence. She warns, however, that focus groups don't produce solutions. Rather, they can help organizations get a better picture of the possibilities and limitations they face. Furthermore, she cautions that people will often talk one way and act another. "Research shows that Americans talk lean but often buy fat. They claim to want dry, dry, dry wine but the reality is their taste runs to sweet."[28]

USING OTHER TECHNIQUES

Many organizations spend a small fortune on surveys and focus groups in an attempt to listen to their customers. But Rekha Balu, of *Fast Company* magazine, would argue that that's not good enough. Focus groups often fail to extract valuable information from customers for several reasons. Customers may want to be "good participants" and respond in the way they think the facilitator would like them to. Or they may be inhibited about expressing their true thoughts and feelings out of concern over how they will be perceived by the others in the group. Or a few strong personalities may dominate the group, discouraging others from sharing their ideas.

Balu recommends trying to get in touch with customers in alternative ways, such as hanging out with them. Instead of bringing customers into an unnatural setting, like a conference room, to listen to them, go where they are and listen to them in their natural environment. In an effort to anticipate the automobile choices of brand-conscious teens (an important customer segment, sometimes called *echo-boomers*), Ford sent a team of engineers and marketers from London to hang out with these future car buyers at the kids' favorite hot spots. With the help of some computer-based tools, the young people were able to help design a car—on the spot—that they would want to buy. "We got a feel for their lifestyle and for what was important to them," explains Andrew Grant, Ford's European consumer marketing insights manager. "We incorporated those insights into some designs and asked, 'Would you want a vehicle like this?' "[29]

Listening to learn from customers often requires listening to more than words. For example, Agilent Technologies wanted to redefine its health-care supply business by serving new markets. Previously Agilent had focused on doctors in hospitals as its customers, but now executives wanted to learn about the needs of nurses, paramedics, and home health aides, who delivered health care in a variety of places. They started by listening to these health-care providers talk about their challenges. What they heard were a lot of comments about the difficulty of listening to patients' hearts and lungs through traditional stethoscopes. It occurred to Agilent that the technology of the traditional stethoscope was more than 100 years old and that much better technology was available to create a new, high-tech stethoscope with amplification up to 14 times higher than traditional models. Agilent heard the need for a new stethoscope, even though no one had actually stated it.[30]

Sometimes, customers have a difficult time stating exactly what they need in the form of a solution because they may think of a product as having only one function and might be unable to imagine using it in any other way. Or they may have multiple needs and see them as contradictory, thus making it difficult to imagine a satisfactory solution. Kimberly-Clark encountered this problem with Huggies diapers. Its customers said that they didn't want their toddlers to wear diapers, but at the same time, they didn't want them to wet the bed, either. The customers could talk about what they *wanted* but couldn't envision a solution. Kimberly-Clark developed the pull-up diaper to solve their contradictory needs.[31]

Anthony Ulwick, CEO of Strategyn and author of *Business Strategy Formulation,* believes that keeping customers talking about what they want or the outcomes they would like, instead of trying to invent solutions, is the best strategy. He developed an outcome-based method of listening to customers that he believes addresses the shortcomings of the typical listening strategies used by organizations. Cordis Corporation, a medical device manufacturer, provides a case in point of this methodology at work. In 1993, Cordis had less than a 1 percent share of the market for the balloons used to open blocked arteries of cardiac patients. Its sales were close to $223 million, and the stock was trading at around $20 per share. Cordis conducted outcome-based marketing research and used the information it acquired to double its sales, gaining a leading position in angioplasty balloons. But Cordis did even more. Listening to doctors talk about what they wanted revealed the need for a product that would prevent arteries from becoming clogged again, so they developed the stent. The stent became "the fastest growing product in medical device history, producing nearly $1 billion in revenue in its first year."[32] The company was acquired by Johnson & Johnson for $109 per share.

Ulwick describes his methodology in five steps.[33]

1. **Plan outcome-based customer interviews.** Customers participating in the interview are carefully selected so that the sample includes only people who actually interact with the product. This is important because part of the planning stage entails learning exactly how the customer uses the product and breaking down that process into steps. Within this group of actual users, the customers selected should be as diverse as possible. For example, Cordis interviewed a diverse set of cardiologists.

2. **Capture desired outcomes.** During this step, the moderator for the interviews listens carefully to what participants have to say. The process starts with participants listing ideas, solutions, or even just adjectives that occur to them when they think about the product. The moderator attempts to keep the customers focused on the process connected to the product and to get them to dig deeply into each of the steps. To do this, a moderator might ask the users a question such as, "Think about what it would be like if the process went perfectly." Or the moderator might ask users to explain why they want things to be as they've described.

   After collecting the information, the moderators sift through the ideas and adjectives and translate them into outcome statements. Well-formulated outcome statements include both the type of improvement desired and some unit of measure for the improvement. The moderator then confirms the translations with the participants. For example, participants in the Cordis study indicated that they wanted the balloon to be "smooth," so the moderator asked them why. The cardiologists explained that they wanted to prevent the device from accidentally dissecting the vessel. From this, the moderator developed the outcome statement "minimize the risk of dissecting a vessel."

3. **Organize the outcomes.** Finally, researchers make a list of all the outcome statements and organize them into groups. Cordis created four categories for its outcomes that represented four stages in the angioplasty process.

4. **Rate outcomes for importance and satisfaction.** The outcomes are then rated by different types of customers for their importance and the degree to which the customers are already satisfied.

5. **Use the outcomes to jump-start innovation.** The results of the survey in step 4 are then analyzed to reveal opportunities for product development.

Using this method of strategic listening, Cordis was able to identify innovative product developments. Between 1994 and 1995, Cordis introduced 12 new angioplasty catheters and grew its market share from 1 percent to nearly 10 percent in the United States.

Listen to This ▼

"Customers have higher expectations and more choices than ever. Which means that you have to listen more closely than ever. Forget building a learning organization. You first have to build a listening organization—a company whose people have their ears to the ground." [34]

—Rekha Balu
Fast Company magazine ▲

The future is sure to bring about innovative ways to listen to customers. Organizations already have Web sites where customers can find contact information. Most offer an e-mail address so that customers can send messages whenever they want. Some companies, such as Pacific Sunwear, have live, online help whenever it's needed, and others have regularly scheduled chats with representatives of the organization. The ease and convenience of electronic communication may increase the likelihood that customers (at least those comfortable with online environments) will make the effort to provide feedback to organizations. Additionally, this type of feedback is unlikely to be structured or led by close-ended questions. Purchasing behavior is another form of feedback that is easier to track, thanks to technology. The technology available today, such as computer barcodes, shopping cards, and devices that track Internet activity, make it easier for interested parties to study purchasing behavior.

Thought Box

What are some of the challenges you face with listening openly to stakeholders outside your organization? Can a customer or client give you too much feedback? How do you respond to feedback from customers or clients who don't understand your company?

LISTENING IN TEAMS

Organizations have long recognized the potential value of self-managed teams. Of course, the true value of teams is often not recognized. When it comes to teamwork, process determines outcome. Teams without an effective manner for members to work together have a diminished chance for success. Five common problems that lead teams to fail include the following:

1. Personality clashes
2. Lack of leadership
3. Communication problems
4. Lack of trust
5. Rush to action

In many ways, these failures can be traced to problems with listening and can be addressed by listening more effectively. High-performing teams have a culture of listening and demonstrate listening behaviors that differ from troubled teams. Training work teams to practice the behaviors exhibited by successful teams can improve their outcomes and help them avoid the commons problems that lead to team failure.

In general, successful teams exercise effective meeting management. Teams work together through meetings, and when they meet, they communicate. Effective meeting management ensures that teams use functional processes for communication. Creating a good climate with a positive, respectful, warm atmosphere encourages communication. Having (at least) an informal agenda for every meeting is important to the successful flow of communication. And a good discussion is more likely if the format of the discussion is established (e.g., go around the table or raise your hand to speak).

Specific recommendations for promoting effective communication and creating high-performing teams include those discussed next.

APPRECIATE DIFFERENCES

Work teams are often created to maximize diversity. You may have a mix of genders, nationalities, and backgrounds on a given team. Diversity slows group progress and makes it more difficult to reach an agreement; however, the outcomes of diverse groups are better than those of highly homogeneous groups. Learning to manage differences is worth the effort required. As long as differences are expected and respected, they can improve the performance of a team.

Teams that are successful spend time getting to know one another and building relationships among the team members. Strengthening the personal connection can help team members accept the differences among them. Getting to know one another a little bit helps develop trust and create positive associations within the team.

Listening Strategy:
Listen to diverse points of view with an open mind and true curiosity. Avoid relying on assumptions that may reflect your own perspective and not the group's. Respond to diverse ideas with respectful feedback.

BE SURE THAT GOALS ARE CLEAR

Research reveals that a common problem for teams is lack of clear understanding as to why the team exists in the first place. In the rush to benefit from self-managed teams, some organizations create teams that do not have a clear purpose.

Teams need to clarify their purpose in the first meetings. Members should discuss the specifics of their goals and objectives to make certain that everyone on the team is thinking about the goals in the same way. For example, your MBA team may have a goal of "doing well on a project." But "doing well" could mean different things to different team members and should be defined more clearly. Teams can benefit from a careful exploration of assumptions about what it means to "participate in meetings" or to "be on time" or "be prepared." Team members are often surprised to find that they interpret these things differently.

Listening Strategy:

Ask clarifying questions and give reflective feedback to ensure that the members of the group are defining words in the same way. Ask questions to discover individual goals that may be at odds with the team goals. Listen nonjudgmentally so that members will feel comfortable expressing their concerns about committing to the team goals.

ASSIGN TEAM ROLES

As teams develop and needs change, team members tend to occupy different roles. For example, leadership may become shared and dependent on the demands of a particular task. However, it is useful in the early stages of team development to discuss who will be responsible for what and to explicitly assign team roles. Research shows that if no formal assignments are made, two roles are most likely to spontaneously emerge: leader and slacker. At the minimum, young teams should consider assigning roles that help ensure the processes in team meetings are effective. Roles that can be helpful when assigned are offered in "Useful Roles to Assign in Teams."

Listening Strategy:

Roles such as facilitator, perception checker, and recorder can contribute to everyone in a team meeting participating fully, the group reaching a common understanding of messages, and the group remembering what was decided. At the minimum, assign the roles of facilitator and recorder. The facilitator will manage group participation so that everyone gets heard. The recorder will create the group memory for meetings and assignments.

ENCOURAGE MORE LISTENING BEFORE ACTING

Teams typically go through predictable phases when completing a project, including stages of defining the problem, producing solutions, evaluating solutions, making decisions, and assigning responsibilities. In each of the phases, discussion is an important part of the team process. However, in their rush to act on their ideas, many teams cut short the discussion and decide what to do before listening to enough discussion. For example, in the problem definition phase of teamwork, many team members arrive at the first meeting with the problem defined in the most obvious way and operate as if that definition is the only one to consider. They may miss the complexity of a problem. If a problem is defined in an overly simplified way, then the solution produced may not address all the issues. In fact, if a problem is defined incorrectly, it may be difficult for the team to produce a solution at all.

Useful Roles to Assign in Teams

Leader
- Guides and energizes team
- Sets the general agenda
- Manages content of meetings
- Handles or assigns administrative details
- Contributes ideas without dominating

Facilitator
- Directs discussion traffic and attention of the group
- Manages process of meetings
- Ensures participation from everyone
- Controls members that tend to dominate conversation
- Protects people from verbal attacks
- Remains neutral
- Keeps team on task
- Intervenes when the meeting is running over a given time limit

Recorder/Perception Checker
- Creates a visual display of information during decision making
- Keeps a record of the meeting
- Writes out key words or phrases that others say
- Asks the group to slow down or asks for help if recording is slowing meeting
- Checks the group's understanding to ensure that everyone is interpreting what is said in the same way
- Summarizes and restates group's conclusions

Devil's Advocate
- Presents opposing viewpoints to make certain that all angles have been considered

Quality Advisor
(This is a role that should be assumed by someone who is good at managing group processes at times when the team seems to be "stuck." The quality advisor remains a neutral observer of the process during a meeting and makes his or her main contributions after the meeting is over.)
- Monitors the team processes and makes suggestions for improving them
- Offers suggestions about project management tools

Listening strategy:
Use verbal behaviors that encourage the exploration of ideas, such as proposing a course of action. Asking clarifying questions to ensure the entire team understands what's been said and encouraging team members to build on one another's ideas is useful. Committing a specified amount of time to discussion (e.g., "Let's discuss each idea for 10 minutes") can promote more listening before action. Engaging these processes is more likely when roles have been assigned to team members. Using a variety of process tools in meetings can encourage more discussion. The more tools you have in your toolbox, the more successful the meetings will be.

SET SOME GROUND RULES

Teams sometimes find it useful to create a contract for the team members that establishes rules for appropriate behavior. Rules involve issues such as arriving for meetings on time, letting the team know in advance of an absence, responding to messages within a specified time limit, and the like. Some teams issue rules about communication and feedback in team meetings, such as avoiding sarcastic remarks and listening respectfully. Establishing rules will create expectations for team members and sensitize them to the importance of the various behaviors for the functioning of the team. Furthermore, the contract can serve as a way to begin a discussion if a team member's behavior is not meeting the group's expectations.

Listening Strategy:

Two important things to do during a discussion with an errant team member are to ask open-ended questions and then to listen nonjudgmentally. You should employ empathic listening if the relationship with the team member has deteriorated to the point of bad feelings. Don't wait to have this discussion. The longer you wait, the harder it will be, because resentment and bad feelings will have grown.

Formats for Producing Solutions That Encourage Listening Before Acting

- **Ordinary group with strong leadership.** The leader structures and leads the discussion.
- **Brainstorming.** Many diverse ideas are generated. Participants are encouraged to piggyback on one another's ideas. Criticism of ideas is not allowed, and self-censoring is strongly discouraged.
- **Reverse brainstorming.** Unlike brainstorming, this technique encourages criticism of ideas. The process begins with listing all things wrong with the process, policy, product, or other item of consideration. Each flaw is then examined individually.
- **Idea-spurring questions.** A series of provocative questions is asked to encourage the production of ideas. For example:

Can we ...	adapt?	substitute?
	modify?	rearrange?
	magnify?	reverse?
	minimize?	combine?

- **Forced relationship technique.** A technique that forces the attributes of one item onto another. (For example, if you are trying to improve coffeemakers, you might compare coffeemakers with alarm clocks. Alarm clocks have alarms. Could a coffeemaker use an alarm? Some alarm clocks are battery operated. Could a coffeemaker be battery operated?)
- **Nominal group technique.** A form of brainstorming with four stages: 1. The problem is stated and participants individually write down alternative solutions. 2. Solutions are shared while a recorder writes them down. 3. Ideas are briefly discussed for clarification. 4. Participants are asked to select the best ideas.

Thought Box

1. What makes working in teams so challenging at times? How can effective listening help?

2. Does your organization provide any team training for employees? What sort of training might help employees listen better in their teams?

LISTENING TO CONFLICT AT THE ORGANIZATIONAL LEVEL

The workplace can be a hotbed for conflict, which is not altogether a bad thing. Constructive conflict that is oriented around work tasks can be helpful in an organization and can lead to better outcomes than those that would otherwise be achieved. Destructive conflict, however, can damage workplace relationships and ultimately hurt an organization's productivity. The parties involved in destructive workplace conflicts can vary. Employees may be in conflict with one another, an employee may be in conflict with an individual manager or "management" in general, and of course, as Howard Guttman points out in his book *When Goliaths Clash*, conflict can occur between senior executives as well.[35]

LISTENING TO EMPLOYEE CONFLICTS

When employees engage in destructive conflicts within organizations, they, at the very minimum, may talk behind the back of the other party. At worst, they may become violent. Nationally, there are 18,000 cases of nonfatal violence in the workplace per week.[36] Many employee conflicts flare up and subside without being noticed by anyone except the parties themselves. At other times, however, conflicts between employees can escalate to the point of becoming a real problem for the company. Other employees can get drawn into the conflict as the parties talk about the conflict, attempting to get support for their side and build opposition to the other party. Conflicts between employees can sour a work environment, dividing employees, creating tension, and distracting people from their work. The conflict can take on a distracting excitement, and employees can become more focused on the developing conflict than on their work.

At this point (or perhaps a little before it), managers may have to intervene in employee conflict. Intervention usually involves bringing in a third party to work with the conflicting parties. A manager can act as a third party, but only if the manager is not personally involved in the conflict, is perceived by the parties as unbiased, and believes himself or herself to be unbiased. If any of these conditions doesn't hold, it is advisable to bring in another third party, which could be someone from human resources or even a professional mediator.

In the event that a manager does want to act as the third party for the conflict, a few important strategies should be implemented. The most important goal for the

Listen to This ▼

"A good manager doesn't try to eliminate conflict; he tries to keep it from wasting the energies of his people. If you're the boss and your people fight with you openly when they think that you are wrong—that's healthy."[37]

—Robert Townsend ▲

manager when meeting with the parties will be to listen and to help the conflicting parties listen well to each other. The manager will need to help the parties reach an understanding of each other's perspective. To achieve this, managers must do several things:

1. **Create an environment that minimizes listening barriers.** The manager will no doubt have the responsibility for setting up the meeting with the parties. Choose a comfortable location where interruptions and distractions will be minimal. A conflict conversation demands 100 percent of the parties' listening energy.

2. **Ask good questions.** Questions should be designed to further the understanding between the parties. Managers must encourage parties to share what is important to them and what they feel they need in order to resolve the conflict. The parties must share their perspective, but in a way that doesn't sound like blaming.

3. **Reframing.** The third party in the conflict must reframe the statements of the parties so that they are positive or neutral. Statements that include extreme generalities like "always" or "never," sarcasm, and negative inferences about motives or intentions should be restated by the third party in more neutral terms.

4. **Give feedback about commonalities and progress.** Parties can often be so upset over issues in a conflict that they fail to see their common ground. For example, parties can have the same goal but disagree on *how* to achieve it. They can lose sight of the goal they share because it is eclipsed by the adversarial relationship they develop over their disagreement. During the conflict conversation, it may be difficult for parties to listen for small progressions they make toward resolution. The third party can listen for these and point them out to the parties.

At one time, the responsibility for dealing with employee conflicts would have fallen on someone in human resources, but the current trend is for this to be taken on by line managers. Although managers may be called upon to settle employee conflicts and can often mediate simple conflicts effectively, a few problems may arise if the reliance on managers is too regular. First, managers may become overly stressed by listening to the woes of employees. And second, when conflicts are complex, managers who have no special training may not be equipped to effectively mediate the conflict.[38]

To prevent these sorts of problems, organizations should have procedures in place for reaching out to professional listeners. Bringing in a professional mediator or facilitator should be considered when conflicts are complex, when they appear to be escalating, or when they appear to be disrupting work. Many organizations that already recognize the value of offering employees access to an outside third party have an Employee Assistance Program. In many cases, these programs provide employees with counseling services that are confidential so that even the company doesn't know which employees are using them. Employees who may be reluctant to go to a counseling service that would be reported to their insurance company are willing to go to EAP counselors. Some organizations make agreeing to visit an EAP counselor when ordered a condition of employment.

LISTENING TO CONFLICTS WITH MANAGEMENT

When the "other party" in an employee conflict is a particular manager or is "management" in general, employees may not feel comfortable directly expressing the conflict because of the power difference. If they feel powerless to directly confront the conflict, they may begin to express the conflict in indirect and subtle ways. They may speak negatively about the manager or the organization as a whole, arrive late for work, take longer than usual to complete a task, call in sick more often, make more mistakes, and the like. In extreme cases, indirect expression may not be subtle: Employees can steal or vandalize.

Even when employees do raise issues with managers, they may do so in an indirect manner. But in an organization that has created a culture of listening, sharing information will be more straightforward. Organizations can encourage a more direct expression of conflict from employees through the following measures:

- **Create a formal system for upward communication.** Organizations benefit from upward communication in numerous ways. Employees can offer insights about the organization that managers can't access. Ways of creating opportunities for organizations to learn from their employees have been discussed previously in this chapter. In cases of conflict communication, the system for upward communication could be modified to improve the outcomes for the particular demands of conflict. A standardized grievance procedure that allows employees to file a grievance about a manager can offer employees a way of raising an issue that they wouldn't be able to raise otherwise. Formal grievance procedures are often reserved for serious concerns about mistreatment, such as sexual harassment or discrimination, and are often accompanied by possibilities of litigation. However, the organization can define the system and how it should be used.
- **Build trust.** Part of the success of any system for upward communication will depend on how a manager reacts to bad news. A willingness to listen will go a long way toward building trust in employees. Employees need to feel that they won't somehow be punished for communicating something that might not be pleasant to hear.
- **Use positive language.** When responding to employee issues or when raising issues, using positive or neutral language will foster an open communication climate.

Managers often have to make unpopular decisions, and sometimes conflict with employees will ensue. One approach to this situation is to be confident in your managerial decision and let time heal things with the employees. But another possibility is listening. It may seem pointless to listen to employees' objections to a decision that you know you aren't able or willing to change, but it is important to recognize that listening does not mean "agreeing." What it does mean, however, is "valuing." When you listen to employee concerns, whether you agree with their views or not, you communicate that you value them, which is sometimes enough to make employees happy. Many employees just want to have a voice in corporate policy and procedure. They don't always expect or need the company to follow what they say; they only want to know that they've been heard.

At the corporate level, when the other party in a conflict is outside the organization, the temptation for many executives is to avoid contact with the customer, clients, investors, or others who are angry. Executives are often advised not to talk about the issue, except possibly to deny liability and denounce the claims of their accusers. They are rarely told to consider crisis communication as a negotiation tool, with an eye toward mutual gains through information sharing. But often, the public, like the individual consumer, wants more than anything else to be heard and to have its concerns acknowledged. According to Lawrence Susskind, one of the founders of the Harvard Program on Negotiation, "It is often possible to acknowledge the public's concerns without accepting responsibility and generating exposure to liability."[39]

Listening effectively to conflict is challenging and often unpleasant for individuals and organizations. But the opportunities it presents make it well worth the effort when the relationships involved are important. It is, again, the first step in resolving conflict. And in certain cases,

---

Thought Box

1. What resources are available at your current or most recent company for employees experiencing conflict? Were they effective? What improvements would you make?

2. What was the attitude of your current or most recent organization toward conflict? How was this communicated?

---

it is, in and of itself, all that is required to resolve conflict. Creating a culture of listening within an organization shatters the image of an impersonal bureaucracy and can only improve relationships with stakeholders, both internal and external.

In this chapter we have explored strategies for listening at the organizational level. As with improving our own personal listening skills, creating change in an organization takes time and commitment, but the benefits clearly make the effort worthwhile. Creating a listening culture is not a panacea for businesses, though. Knowing what your customers want won't solve your problems if your pricing strategy is way off. But, as we have seen, the business world offers many examples of organizations reaping rewards from practicing effective listening. Whatever your position in your organization, exhibiting effective listening skills can affect outcomes and improve relationships with your internal and external stakeholders.

Becoming an effective listener is not a goal that you set for yourself, achieve, and check off the to-do list. Effective listening is ongoing commitment that is redefined and renewed with each interaction. No one will ever be an effective listener all the time, and you would be well-advised to run from anyone who promises to make you one. Reading a textbook, such as this one, or participating in a workshop will not even automatically make you a better listener. Any listening training will improve your listening only to the extent that you continually exert the effort necessary to listen well. This textbook has provided you with information about listening barriers and described some techniques for overcoming them. But perhaps even more important than offering you these tools for improving your ability to listen, we hope this book has given you added motivation to listen well by pointing out the many benefits associated with effective listening for you as an individual and as a manager.

DISCUSSION QUESTIONS

1. Do different formal feedback systems work more or less well at different levels of an organization? What types of feedback systems would you recommend at different levels to encourage feedback from all levels in the company?

2. Imagine that you have recently joined an organization with a closed communication climate in your new department. As head of the department, how can you create and communicate a culture of listening?

3. What is the mission statement of your current or most recent organization? Is listening effectively a part of achieving this mission? How could the organization use listening in pursuit of its mission?

4. How can managers create a healthy attitude toward conflict within their organization? How can managers help employees deal with conflict in a constructive manner?

5. How do you as a manager know when it's time to intervene in an employee conflict? How do you know when you need to get outside help?

ENDNOTES

1. "Panera Bread—Company History." Retrieved October 20, 2004, from http://www.panerabread .com/about_co_history.aspx.
2. S. Kirsner, "Four Leaders You Need to Know," *Fast Company* no. 91 (February 2005): 68.
3. "Panera Bread Introduces the Nation to Great Tasting, Lower-Carb Bakery Breads." Retrieved June 2, 2004, from http://thesoydailyclub.com/Food/lowCarbbread06042004.asp.
4. "St. Louis Fine Restaurant Guide—Restaurant News." Retrieved August 5, 2003, from http://www .diningstl.com/News082403.htm.
5. "Concerns Raised that Changes in NASA Won't Last," CNN.com, August 26, 2003. Available at http://www.cnn.com/2003/TECH/space/08/26/sprj.colu.shuttle.report/.
6. L. Stark, "Not Just the Foam," ABCnews.com, June 11, 2003. Available at: http://www.globalsecurity .org/org/news/2003/030611-shuttle-report01.htm.
7. J. H. Baker, "Are You Listening?" *WeLead Online Magazine* (2003). Available at http://www .leadingtoday.org/Onmag/feb03/hb-feb03.html.
8. P. Derringer, "Go Team," *The Manufacturer*. Available at http://www.conquestbm.com/manusnew/ hr/hr_go-team.htm. Retrieved March 1, 2004.
9. C. W. Downs and A. D. Adrian, *Assessing Organizational Communication: Strategic Communication Audits* (New York: Guilford Press, 2004).
10. "How Much Money Are You Losing from Ideas You're Not Getting?" HRmadeEasy e-Newsletter (2004). Available at http://www.biztrain.com/motivation/stories/losing.htm.
11. "How Much Money Are You Losing?" *supra* n. 10.
12. F. Turner, "Employee Suggestions Contribute to the Bottom Line," *The CEO Refresher* (2001). Available at http://www.refresher.com/!suggestion3.html.
13. F. Turner, "Employee Suggestions Are Profitable—Do You Listen?" *The CEO Refresher* (2001). Available at http://www.refresher.com/!suggestion2.html.
14. J. Guiniven, *Public Relations Tactics* 7, no. 2 (February 2000), 22.
15. J. Moore Jr., "Supervisors Learn to Listen to Employees," *Supervision* 57, no. 4 (April 1996): 11.
16. Ibid.
17. D. Domeyer, "Do Bosses Heed Employee Suggestions," *USA Today Magazine* (March 2001), Available at http://www.24hourscholar.com/p/articles/mi_m1272/is_2670_129/ai_72272556.
18. Guiniven, *supra* n. 14.
19. L. Michaud, "How to Turn the Tables on Employee Turnover," Career Journal Europe.com (2004). Available at http://www.careerjournaleurope.com/hrcenter/ipma/200104013-ipma-michaud.html. Retrieved March 27, 2004.
20. "Sam Walton Quotes." Retrieved June 25, 2004, from http://www.brainyquote.com/quotes/authors/ s/sam_walton.html.
21. M. McGraw. "Women in Leadership," presentation at Mendoza College of Business, University of Notre Dame, April 23, 2004.
22. M. Buckingham and C. Coffman, *First, Break all the Rules* (New York: Simon & Schuster, 1999).
23. Ibid.
24. A. Caborn, "A Healthy Exchange," *Employee Benefits* (May 2003): 26–29.
25. R. White, "I Love Complaints," *Credit Union Management* (January 2003): 46–47.
26. B. Goebert, *Beyond Listening* (New York: John Wiley & Sons, 2002).

27. Ibid.
28. Ibid., 69.
29. R. Balu, "Listen Up!" *Fast Company* no. 34 (May 2000): 304.
30. Ibid.
31. D. Leonard, "The Limitations of Listening," *Harvard Business Review* (January 2002): 93.
32. A. W. Ulwick, " Turn Customer Input into Innovation," *Harvard Business Review* (January 2002): 91–97.
33. Ibid.
34. Balu, *supra* n. 29.
35. H. M. Guttman, *When Goliaths Collide: Managing Executive Conflict to Build a More Dynamic Organization* (New York: AMACOM, 2003).
36. National Institute for Occupational Safety and Health, "Violence in the Workplace" (July 1996). Available at http://www.cdc.gov/niosh/violfwd.html.
37. "Robert Townsend Quotes." Retrieved June 25, 2004, from http://www.brainyquote.com/quotes/authors/r/robert_townsend.html.
38. A. Caborn, "A Healthy Exchange," *Employee Benefits* (May 2003): 26–29.
39. L. Susskind, "When an Angry Public Wants to be Heard," *Negotiation* 1, no. 1 (November 2003).

A CASES

AMAZON MARKETPLACE: IT'S A JUNGLE OUT THERE

BACKGROUND

In the summer of 2004, Kate Lindsey's father helped his daughter prepare for the fall semester by ordering all her textbooks online, with the belief that she would have them before she left for campus.[1] Because not all Web sites carried the books she needed (or had the least expensive price), her dad ordered from several vendors. One book was from Zoe's Books,[2] a vendor through the Amazon.com marketplace, where anyone can sell books. That particular book did not arrive before Kate left for campus in August, so her father called the post office, filed a change of address form for Kate, and asked the postal service to forward the book to her once it arrived.

However, the post office failed to forward the textbook, and instead it was delivered to Kate's home. When it arrived, her dad took it to the post office and asked them to mail it to her dorm address, which they said they would. Two weeks later, however, the book arrived back at her home in Chesapeake, Virginia. Once again, her dad took the package to the post office and explained the situation; the postmaster said he would personally see to it that the book arrived at the campus. This time, the book didn't arrive at either address.

THE PAPER TRAIL

The book never arrived, so Kate's father sent e-mail to both Amazon and Zoe's Books to find out whether the book had been returned to the originating address. Zoe's Books never replied; Amazon did, stating that someone from Amazon would discuss the situation with the vendor (Zoe's Books) and recommend a refund. Only after Amazon contacted Zoe's Books did the company send a reply. In a curt and defensive e-mail message, the owner of Zoe's Books said, "We did our end of the deal. . . . You ordered a book [sic] we sent it . . . and it never arrived. How is that our fault?"

The e-mail chain continued, and with each reply, the owner became more curt, more accusatory, and more rude. She used phrases such as, "Lets [sic] not play dumb," "you screwed up," and "its [sic] in your hands [sic] not ours." At the third tier of the exchange, Kate's father copied Amazon and told the owner that she was rude and unprofessional and that he would not recommend her business to others. Immediately put on the defensive, she seemed intent on proving that her business was successful and that she was not at fault, stating, "I have learned nothing from this issue."

THE E-MAIL EXCHANGES

To: xxxxxxxxxx@xxxxx.xxx
Sent: Thursday, October 28, 2004 6:05 AM
Subject: Scott Lindsey order

Hi,
I ordered, *Why We Get Sick: The New Science of Darwinian Medicine* back in August, from Amazon. It came to my house . . . and I took it to the post office to forward to my daughter at college. It was returned to my address, so I took it to the PO again and they assured me they would get it to my daughter. It's been over a month now and she still hasn't received it. Now I'm thinking maybe this book was returned to you.

Please call me at xxx.xxx.xxxx, or email me at yyyyyyyyyy@yyyyy.yyy so I can either reorder with a new address, or so you can credit my account.

Thanks,
Scott Lindsey

From: xxxxxxxxxx@xxxxx.xxx
Sent: Thursday, October 28, 2004 7:44 PM
To: yyyyyyyyyy@yyyyy.yyy
Subject: Re: Scott Lindsey order

Why would you put a claim in about your order asking for your money back when you received the book? We did our end of the deal. I bet you didn't even bother to rewrap it and just wrote on the paper it was wrapped in. How is this our fault, in any way? You ordered the book, we sent it, you made an attempt to send it onto someone else and it never arrived. How is that our fault? By the way, we have already sent your e-mail you sent us to Amazon.

Zoe's Books

To: xxxxxxxxxx@xxxxx.xxx
Sent: Thursday, October 28, 2004 7:35 PM
Subject: RE: Scott Lindsey order

You're right—you did your end of the deal. It's not your fault. I have no problem with you. I'm just trying to find out where the book is. Did USPS return it to you? I don't have it, and my daughter doesn't have it. I thought maybe the PO tried to "return to sender." Did it come back to you?

Scott Lindsey

From: xxxxxxxxxx@xxxxx.xxx
Sent: Friday, October 29, 2004 10:12 AM
To: yyyyyyyyyy@yyyyy.yyy
Subject: Re: Scott Lindsey order

No, we did not get the book back here, but you still put a claim into Amazon. What does Amazon have anything to do with the USPS? Why did Amazon send us a harassing email saying refund the money if we did not send it to you? Why didn't you write back about the claim you put into Amazon? Lets not play dumb, you screwed up and your looking to get your money back Bottom line, its in your hands not ours or Amazons its up to you and the post office.

To: xxxxxxxxxx@xxxxx.xxx
Cc: zzzzzzzzzz@amazon.com
Sent: Friday, October 29, 2004 10:17 AM
Subject: Amazon order

Zoe,
You are one caustic, contentious individual. I can't imagine how you run a business with the poor people skills that you demonstrate here.

If I were Amazon, I would sever all ties with your company. I would not want to be associated with a subcontractor who interacts with customers the way you do.

I have been professional and unemotional in my emails to you and to Amazon. Fortunately, Amazon was professional and courteous in their reply. Unlike you, Amazon realizes the key to future business success is customer satisfaction. I will never recommend you—not because you didn't deliver a quality product, but rather because of the rudeness you show when asked a very simple question.

I am sending a copy of this email chain to Amazon, for use as they see fit. Although this incident is not their fault either, they are taking a much more mature and magnanimous course of action. Unlike you, Amazon responded quickly to my email (you responded only after Amazon contacted you; my bet is that you would have ignored my email otherwise).

I've learned three things from all this:
1. Don't forward a book without re-wrapping it (my fault).
2. Amazon is a good company.
3. Zoe's Books is not.

Finally, I am also sending this e-mail chain to my daughter at the University of Notre Dame. She's a marketing major. I'm sure she will be interested in using this information for her senior project: "How to fail at business without really trying."

Scott Lindsey

From: xxxxxxxxxx@xxxxx.xxx
Sent: Friday, Oct 29, 2004 6:38 PM
To: yyyyyyyyyy@yyyyy.yyy

Hi There:

The only reason we were up in arms about this issue is because we received an email saying refund your money because you did not receive the book and you had put in a claim. You are not the first person who has tried to do this with us. We have lost a lot of money in the past because a lot of people what something for nothing. Put yourself in our shoes for a minute you bought the book received the book and then wrote us and soon after and then put a claim for a refund. Would you have been okay with that? I asked, "Why?" Just to let you know we have been very successful with our book store and maybe if you didn't not put a claim in we wouldn't be in dismay. I learned nothing from this issue because we have gone through this before too many times. One other thing: why haven't you answered why you put a claim in, what reason?

Zoe's Books

From: yyyyyyyyyy@yyyyy.yyy
Date: Friday, October 29, 2004 6:04 PM
To: xxxxxxxxxx@xxxxx.xxx

Subject: Re: Amazon order

I never put in a claim. I wrote Amazon and told them the same thing I told you—that I tried to forward the book to my daughter at college and she never got it. I don't have it. I thought maybe USPS returned it to sender (you). I'm not trying to get something for nothing. I am willing to reorder (with a different address), or, since shipping costs more than the book itself, if it came back to you I was willing to let it stay with you and get a credit on my credit card. As it stands, my daughter has to write a paper on the book next week, and so she's going to go buy it herself, somewhere in Indiana. If there is any fault, it's mine for not knowing I had to re-wrap the book before forwarding. I would have thought the PO would have told me that, but they didn't. I'm just trying to find out where the book is.

I never expected to get a refund, but Amazon, being the great company they are, decided a whopping $7.24 is worth keeping a customer happy, even though none of this is Amazons'—or your—fault. You should adopt that concept.

What disappoints me about you is your attitude. You are accusatory and jump to conclusions without getting the facts. All you needed to say, in your first email to me, was, "I'm sorry Mr. Lindsey, we don't have the book here, but if it shows up I'll let you know and you can decide what you want to do."

DISCUSSION QUESTIONS

1. Three companies (the United States Postal Service, Amazon.com, and Zoe's Books) and a consumer were the players in this case. How would you evaluate the listening effectiveness for each of these parties?

2. What could the different companies have done to improve their listening, overall communication effectiveness, and final outcome in this case?

3. How should Amazon respond to Zoe's Books? What responsibility, if any, do they have for the behavior of their marketplace sellers? Does Amazon's relationship with the customer end at the point of the transaction with a marketplace seller? Who should listen to customer complaints, Amazon, the marketplace seller, or both?

KMART CORPORATION: A RETAILER'S DILEMMA

"You want to know what's wrong with Kmart? I can tell you what's wrong with Kmart." Kara listened to her mother and immediately regretted wondering aloud why the Kmart had closed as they had driven past the large, empty building. Since Kara had moved out on her own, she had frequently shopped at Kmart and relied on it to have nice-looking items for her apartment at a price even she could afford. Now, three of the four stores in her community were closed.

"The last time I went into Kmart," Kara's mother continued, "I just wanted to run in and run out, but I wound up standing in line for over 15 minutes. I got in line behind two women who only had a few items, but the checkout girl had *all kinds* of problems. First, every time she scanned something and then moved the item to put it in the bag, the scanner would read it again." Kara's mom acted out the movements as she spoke, "And then she would have to stop ringing things up and void the item out. This happened over and over again." Kara's mom shook her head, "Now, I don't know if the scanner was just too sensitive or if this girl wasn't trained well, but the whole thing was just ridiculous and time consuming.

"But that wasn't the worst of it. The woman right in front of me had picked up a few sale items. She was watching the screen and stopped the checker when her sale items showed up at regular price. Then the checker explained that the cash register doesn't show the sale price on the screen, but it will show on the receipt *at the end of the transaction when the register prints one*. What were they thinking?" Kara's mother exclaimed excitedly.

She was on a roll now, and nothing was going to stop her, so Kara just listened. "People come to Kmart for low prices and sales. It doesn't seem like it would take a rocket scientist to figure out that people are going watch the prices as they go through the checkout. And if they see their sales items ringing up for regular price, they're going to think something is wrong. How many times a day do you think those cashiers have to explain to people how their system works?"

"And that's not the only problem," she said. "I happen to know that if something rings up wrong or you change you mind about something and the transaction has already been completed, the checker can't just give you back your money. You have to go over to the customer service counter, wait in line again, and then have someone help you. If anyone at the corporate offices of Kmart had ever asked a customer, they would have known what was going wrong with their stores."

Her mother seemed to be finished, so Kara responded, "You have a point, but surely not all Kmart stores would have the exact same machines, and yet stores closed all over the country."

"Well, you know, they have a reputation for not being really clean and not keeping their shelves stocked. It's hard to compete with stores like Wal-Mart and Target when you have that working against you. But, who knows? Now with Sears in the picture, we may see a lot of positive changes in Kmart."

Kara hoped that some things didn't change too much. She still wanted to be able to buy the brands she liked and couldn't get anywhere else, like Martha Stewart Everyday and Thalia Sodi at low prices. Kara also wondered if there was more to this story than her mother knew. What else went wrong at Kmart?

KMART: THE SHORT STORY

Kmart's origins date back to 1899, when Sebastian Spering Kresge opened a downtown Detroit store where everything was priced at 5 or 10 cents. He believed that if consumers were offered products they need at a price they could afford, they would keep coming back. In the early years, this simple philosophy worked well for Kresge. By 1912, he was able to expand to 85 stores.

Over the next several decades, the company continued to do well and grow at a modest rate but, by the 1950s, it became clear that increased competition in retailing would force the Kresge company to make some significant changes. The company looked to their new president, Harry Cunningham, appointed in 1959, to guide them in a another direction.

It was under Cunningham's leadership that the first Kmart store was opened in 1962, in Garden City, Michigan, and 17 more stores were opened in that same year. Over the next 15 years, Kmart opened hundreds of stores at a rapid rate, even making history in 1976 by opening 17 million square feet of retail space in a single year. By 1977, almost 95 percent of the S.S. Kresge Company's sales were generated by Kmart stores. As a natural response to this development, the company officially changed its name to Kmart Corporation and 10 years later sold all the remaining Kresge stores.

In the past decade, Kmart felt the squeeze from some highly successful competitors. Other retailers adopted the philosophy of offering consumers what they need at low prices, and some did a better job of it than Kmart. Wal-Mart, a formidable opponent in the world of discount merchandising, has become known as the retailer with the lowest price, well-stocked shelves, and the widest selection of merchandise. Target, another major competitor for Kmart, has positioned itself as the place to go for low prices on trendy, stylish items.

In an effort to catch up to the competition, Kmart attempted some major innovations. In 1996, it added a "pantry" department to its stores, selling frequently purchased consumer goods. To reflect this change, the remodeled stores were renamed Big Kmart. In 1999, Kmart carved out an Internet presence that was far ahead of Wal-Mart, with BlueLight.com. But these changes weren't enough.

In May 2000, Chuck Conaway was appointed chairman and chief executive officer of Kmart. Conaway was a rising star at CVS, and though he had one bankruptcy behind him at Reliable Drugs Store (he left the position of CEO only months before the company filed), the board saw him as a passionate and energetic man who could step up the pace of change at Kmart. Besides, he was a hometown boy with degrees from Michigan State and the University of Michigan. The board was so enthusiastic about their choice that Conaway was offered the position before some of the members had even met him. They thought they had made an excellent decision. They were wrong.

Just days after taking office, Conaway had the portraits of his predecessors removed from his office and the auditorium. A sculpture known as "the Corporate Head" that had stood before the corporate headquarters for decades was hauled away on Conaway's orders. He attempted to motivate employees with shouted speeches delivered from atop a desk and with weekly, sometimes rambling phone messages. He attempted to address Kmart's reputation for poor service by visiting stores. However, while there he was perceived as arrogant and ordered store managers around to the point that many of them quit in frustration.

In the summer of 2001, Kmart made an attempt to compete with Wal-Mart on price with a program known as "BlueLight Always." As part of this effort, the company purchased $850 million of inventory, but it did so without discussing with Kmart's treasury officials whether or not the company had the money for these purchases. In fact, the price war was waged without analyzing the viability of the program and without considering the fact that Kmart was spending millions on modernizing its stores and didn't have the finely tuned distribution system of Wal-Mart. Ultimately, the program failed, and Kmart lost millions in store signs, advertisements, and leftover merchandise.

It was becoming increasingly clear to top executives that the company was in trouble, their stock options weren't worth much, and they could be fired at any time if something didn't improve. In an effort to retain leadership and provide stability for the company, 25 executives received retention loans totaling $28 million. These were loans that did not have to be paid back if the executives were fired.

Kmart endeavored to turn the tide by cutting its advertising budget and attempting to increase vendor rebates paid for placing merchandise on choice shelves. In a desperate move, executives launched "Project Slow It Down," which reduced or stopped payments to suppliers. But none of the efforts was successful.

In the fall of 2001, Kmart reported losses and a decline in sales. On January 2, 2002, a report from Wayne Hood, an industry expert at Prudential Securities, warned that Kmart could be facing bankruptcy. A week later, an anonymous group of employees from Kmart's finance division registered a complaint with the SEC, stating their belief that Kmart's books had been misstated and distorted. "Something is very wrong at Kmart Corporation," they charged.

On January 22, 2002, Kmart petitioned a federal judge for reorganization under Chapter 11 of the United States Bankruptcy Code. On March 8, Conaway announced the closing of 284 of Kmart's money-losing stores. On March 11, Conaway was replaced by Jim Adamson, a member of Kmart's board since 1996, and Julian C. Day was named president and chief operating officer. On January 14, 2003, Kmart issued a press release announcing its plans to close 323 of its underperforming stores as part of its objectives in emerging from Chapter 11. On January 19, Julian Day was promoted to CEO.

On May 6, 2003, after achieving its key objectives, Kmart emerged from Chapter 11. A short time later, on March 24, 2005, Kmart Holding Corporation and Sears, Roebuck and Co. completed the merger that was announced on November 17, 2004. The combined companies, named Sears Holdings Corporation, is the country's third largest retailer, with 3,500 stores in the United States.

The executives of Sears Holdings point to the opportunities that the merger creates to give customers greater access to their exclusive brands and to help Sears achieve its strategy of stores outside of malls. But analysts are not sure what to expect. They ask the following questions:

1. What will the brands stand for? (If Wal-Mart competes principally on price and Target competes on brand and relatively low prices, how will Kmart and Sears compete in the future?)

2. Who will be the major competitors?
3. Will the chains mix brands? Is this a good idea?
4. Will new concepts be developed for the stores?
5. Will current, loyal customers remain customers?
6. Will Sears really be able to attract new customers?

DISCUSSION QUESTIONS

1. What internal and external listening errors were made at Kmart in the 1990s? When the top-level executives in the company are not listening leaders, is there anything that can be done to improve listening effectiveness?

2. Consider the six questions put forth by analysts. How can you use listening strategies to address these six concerns?

3. What recommendations do you have for the leadership of Sears Holdings Corporation to create a strong combined culture for the merged companies?

REFERENCES

"Kmart and Sears Complete Merger to Form Sears Holdings Corporation," press release (March 24, 2005). Available at http://www.kmartcorp.com/corp/story/pressrelease/news/pr050324a.stm.

"About Kmart." Retrieved April 4, 2005, from http://www.kmartcorp.com/corp/story/general/corporate_history.stm.

J. Dixon, "The Fall of Kmart: Enriched Ex-CEO Left Company Struggling; New Man in Charge Vows Full Inquiry and Says Kmart Will Rebound," *The Detroit Free Press* (July 2, 2002). Available at http://www.freep.com/money/business/kmart2_20020702.htm.

K. Dybis, "How 'Frat Boys' Drove Kmart to Ruin," *The Detroit News* (January 26, 2003). Available at http://www.detnews.com/2003/business/0301/27/a01-69100.htm.

B. Horowitz, "Will Kmart Walk Away a Winner with Sears Deal?" *USA Today* (November 22, 2004). Available at http://www.usatoday.com/money/industries/retail/2004-11-17-kmart-sears-cover_x.htm.

SMARTART: WHO'S LISTENING TO THE CUSTOMER?

SmartArt is a small advertising company that produces socially responsible advertising (meaning that it does not produce ads for products deemed harmful to society or use potentially harmful images in its ads). Advertising is a highly creative and competitive field. In an attempt to gain a competitive edge, SmartArt assigns all clients to work teams. The agency has a policy that each team has one person designated as the account manager, who handles all direct communication with the clients. SmartArt thinks speaking to the same person at the agency increases clients' confidence and trust.

THE CHARACTERS

Jane: Jane is the account manager for her team. She has been with SmartArt for more than 10 years. She has an associate's degree in business and has worked her way up from a clerical position to account manager. In part, her success is a result of her follow-through; she does what she says she's going to. Jane is a "by-the-book" sort of person. Her clients like dealing with her because they know what to expect. Her team, on the other hand, appreciates the fact that they can rely on her but find her a little rigid. They would like her to be a little more flexible about things, and they sometimes feel she misses the forest for the trees.

Paul: Paul is the creative element on Jane's team. He is very talented in both his artwork and verbal expression. He has been with the organization for a year. He was a double major in college with a degree in business and fine art. Like many creative people, Paul's work style is a bit spontaneous and sporadic. When he's inspired, he does great work. When he's not, his work is a little flat. His teammates appreciate his creative genius (and they really do think he has genius), but they wish he were more linear in his work schedule. Occasionally, the team has been pushed uncomfortably close to a deadline, waiting for Paul to deliver on his promise of a great idea.

Pat: Pat is one of the partners at the agency. The agency structure has teams assigned to partners. Jane's and Paul's team is assigned to her. Pat knows that teams inevitably experience conflict, and she has a healthy respect for how conflict can improve the team's performance and strengthen the relationships among the team members. She also recognizes that when conflicts become destructive, the team, the clients, and the agency suffer.

THE CRITICAL INCIDENT

Jane answered her phone, and on the line was one of her new clients. "I don't know what's going on, but I just spent nearly an hour on the phone with your creative director talking about the print ads that we already discussed. I thought you were supposed to be handling all of that! I don't have time to tell *you* what I want, only to have to turn around and tell it all over again to somebody else."

Jane was furious. Paul had apparently gone around her and contacted the client on his own. And that was the worst thing he could have done with this client. The client sold hardware and fasteners to manufacturers. He wanted advertising to place in trade journals and guidebooks for trade shows. Describing his fasteners was about as exciting and creative as he cared to get, and the edginess of the work in Paul's portfolio made him uncomfortable from the start. He had gone with the agency because he was confident in Jane, and she assured him that Paul could produce something that would meet his needs. Jane could sense that now the client's confidence in her and the entire agency was shaken. She was particularly upset that Paul would jeopardize the account after she had worked so hard to sell him to a client who didn't really want him.

After Jane hung up the phone, she took a few deep breaths and headed for Paul's office. He was sitting at his computer and looked up at her as she came in.

Jane: Why in the world did you call ZB Fasteners? You've managed to get Bill so upset, he's ready to move to another agency. I can't believe you would do this to the team.

Paul: Look, I just wanted to talk to the guy.

Jane: It's pretty simple Paul, you aren't supposed to call the client. I speak to the client, not you.

Paul: You know what Jane, that's fine. Whatever.

Jane: (offended by his response) Yes, I know it's fine. It's the policy and it's been the policy since before you were here.

Jane left Paul's office angrier than she was when went in, and now Paul was angry as well.

PAUL'S REACTION

Paul had nothing more to say to Jane but had plenty to say to Pat. He was tired of Jane's controlling style. It was her controlling nature that made it necessary for him to call the client in the first place. Although it is true that company policy stated only one person from the team should serve as the primary contact for clients, other teams had team and client meetings, where all the members of the team got to interact with clients. Jane rarely invited any team members to meetings with clients, and no team members except Jane had met anyone from ZB.

When Jane originally described what the client wanted to Paul, he thought he understood it pretty well. He produced a series of print ads he thought were right on target—but they weren't. The client hadn't liked them and had rejected the entire series. Jane had come back to Paul with some feedback from ZB—and a demand for speed. The client had some important trade shows coming up soon and needed to have the ads for the programs done quickly. They didn't have time for another "do-over," so Paul called the client. He needed to be clear about what they wanted and to get Bill's reaction to his initial ideas before he wasted time on something that wouldn't work. He also thought he might be able to talk Bill into accepting ads that had a little more excitement and edge.

Paul felt that if Jane hadn't been so controlling and had let the team meet with the client in the first place, he would have understood the client's needs from the start and would not have had to make the call.

Paul was talented and knew it. He had chosen SmartArt because he respected its mission, but he knew he had standing offers at other agencies. He had already been thinking that Jane's work style was tough for him to deal with. She never gave him any recognition or showed appreciation for his work. Jane was particularly narrow in her thinking and was always focused on schedules and budgets.

He needed to talk to Pat. He would insist upon moving to a different team, and if that weren't possible, he would very likely quit.

PAT'S RESPONSE

Pat was working and enjoying the day when her contentment was interrupted by Paul bursting into her office. He was visibly upset. He began to complain about Jane's controlling style and said he couldn't work with her anymore.

Pat just listened. She tried not to form too much of an opinion of the problem before hearing Jane's side of things. After Paul left, she called Jane.

Jane was surprised when she answered the phone and Pat was on the line—and livid when Pat explained she wanted to see her regarding some things that Paul had brought to her attention. After Paul violated company policy, he had the audacity to complain to Pat. It was lucky for Paul that he wasn't in the hall as Jane walked to Pat's office.

When Jane arrived at Pat's office, she was hardly able to contain her anger.

Pat: So Jane, what's going on with you and Paul?

Jane: Well, right now it's damage control. I'm trying to control the damage that he's trying to do.

Pat: What happened?

Jane then told Pat her side of the story. After Jane left, Pat had several concerns. She didn't want to lose Paul, a talented, creative person, but moving him to another team would be complicated. Because clients were handled by teams, moving Paul meant a whole group of clients would lose their creative lead, and whole different set of clients would have a new one. At the same time, she wanted Jane's team to work well together. Finally, she definitely didn't want to lose a new client.

Pat decided to bring Paul and Jane together for a meeting. She planned to act as a mediator. In her position as partner she had some experience with tough negotiations. She planned to approach this meeting as she would any other negotiation, with one major difference. In this case, the parties weren't going to be negotiating about price or cost; rather, they would be negotiating about how they should treat each other and how things should be done.

THE MEETING

As the meeting began, Pat was thrown a little by how quickly things turned nasty. Jane began with her side of the story.

Jane: Well, as you already know, Paul went behind my back and made me look like an incompetent idiot to the client. And now, if we lose the account. . . .

Paul: Wait a minute, if we lose the account, it won't be because I talked to him, it'll be because I didn't talk to him *soon* enough. You should have let me talk to him before I did the first ad series. Then it would have been done right.

Jane: We have the policy of one person talking to the client for a reason. . . .

Paul: The problem is that you have control issues. Other teams meet with clients, but you act like we're going to embarrass you.

Jane: That's not true. But what you did today did embarrass me.

Paul: Look, I was just trying to help. I think you're overreacting and getting a little overemotional.

Jane: *You're* the one overreacting. I'm not threatening to quit, and I didn't run to Pat like a spoiled child.

The meeting was going nowhere fast, and Pat needed to intervene. But where and how should she start?

DISCUSSION QUESTIONS

1. What listening barriers are likely to exist between Jane and Paul?

2. How much does personality have to do with this conflict? How can you help employees with different personalities listen to each other?

3. Is there a difference between what the parties are saying they want and what they really want? How can you help them people communicate their true needs, which may be different from what they communicate directly with their words?

4. What sources of power do the parties have? How will their power affect their listening?

5. Are there situational or structural factors that contributed to this conflict? Could those be changed and the meeting with Pat be avoided? What are the advantages and disadvantages of this approach?

6. Are the parties making unjustified inferences (committing the fundamental attribution error)? How will that affect their ability to listen?

7. What communication mistakes are the parties making as they talk about the conflict? How will these affect their ability to listen to each other?

8. How should Pat have prepared for the meeting? How can she promote good listening between Jane and Paul?

ROLE PLAY INSTRUCTIONS

To perform the role play, participants should assume the role of Jane, Paul, or Pat. The scene should be the meeting among the three characters that begins at the end of this case. Pat should attempt to facilitate listening and effective communication between Paul and Jane.

ENDNOTES

1. This case is part of a paper titled "Listening Organization," written by Kate Lindsey in November 2004, and is used with her permission.
2. The vendor's name and identifying information have been changed.

INDEX